FOREWARD

John Wesley Wright was my great, great grandfather. He was called "Devil" John. The exact reason for this dubious designation is something that, I believe, can only be ascertained by examining his life as a whole. The title "Devil" was not a complimentary one given by people of the 19th century. The infamous "Devil" Anse Hatfield, head of the Hatfield clan in the celebrated Hatfield-McCoy Feud, would be a prime example. Devil John, however, may have been the exception to the rule. To many he was actually a hero, to others . . . he was just plain evil. The reader will have to reach their own conclusion. By the way, Devil John held a passionate hatred for his northern neighbor, Devil Anse. As for why he felt this way is never mentioned, but it would be likely that Devil John would've sided with the Kentucky McCoys, as he was a Kentuckian by birth.

Here is the "crux of the biscuit." Many books, fiction and nonfiction, (nonfiction that turns out to be fiction) and articles of these same types about Devil John are abundant in libraries, bookstores, newspapers, genealogical works, local histories and online Publications. That being said, there does not exist (in my opinion) even one unbiased, historically accurate and comprehensive (cradle to grave) biography of this extraordinary man

What does exist are two works that are purported to be biographies of Devil John. The problem with these is twofold. They are both filled with historical inaccuracies, and (for vastly different reasons) depict their subject as fancifully as the Dime Novels of yesteryear portrayed the heroes and outlaws of the Old West. The best known of these is "Devil John Wright of the Cumberlands" written by Devil John's son (and my great uncle) William T. "Chid" Wright, which he self-published in 1970 and is currently administered by his estate. This is a wonderful book to read. My autographed copy is among my most treasured possessions, but it is not a historically accurate work and is, understandably, very biased in its presentation. This book is, for the most part, a chronologically arranged collection of stories and remembrances written by a fiercely loyal, loving son about his famous Dad and sweetly dedicated to his "father's works". In my opinion it is an extraordinary memoir, but falls short of being a comprehensively researched, historically accurate biography. It is what it is, and as stated, it's a wonderful read.

The other of these publications is a book titled "Bad John Wright The Law of Pine Mountain", reprinted in 1997 by Overmountain Press in Johnson City, Tennessee, and written by the late Philip K. Epling. This book is, to me, confounding in its huge amount of historical inaccuracies and its portrayal of Devil John is akin to the gunslingers in a bad Western matinee movie.

Epling begins the book with giving the wrong year of Devil John's birth. He claims that John's father captured the man that would, in later life, become Devil John's nemesis, Clabe Jones. The narrative continues with Clabe stealing a horse from the teenaged John, making good his escape. It was this event that Epling claims was the original cause of the Wright-Jones Feud that would play out twenty five years later. The text continues with this event causing young

John to immediately go to the county seat and join the Confederate Army. Epling relates that John, having been in the service for some length of time, saves the life of Talt Hall from a Confederate Captain (bent on killing him as an accused "bushwhacker") by assuring the officer that John would see to it that Talt would join him in the cavalry company John had already seen action in. This all sounds good, but based on the existing historical records, it' hard to see how any of it's true!

History records that the seminal events leading to the Wright-Jones Feud would not occur until years after the war was over. Furthermore, the records that exist to this day plainly show that Thomas Talton Hall and John Wright were signed-in to their cavalry company together . . . on the exact same day   These and a myriad other mistakes of historicity are combined with page after page of dramatic and somewhat campy dialogue, essentially quotes by Devil John and others, with a conspicuous lack of citation for the sources of these quotes. It's possible that Mr. Epling wasn't going to let actual history get in the way of a good story. As stated, the whole book comes off like an old time Dime Novel about the Wild West, and is disappointing, at best, for someone wishing to simply know the real history of Devil John Wright. In my opinion it's a swing . . . and a miss!

Beyond all of this, is the way Devil John is consistently portrayed in virtually everything printed about him. He is always either romanticized or demonized   In other words, he seems to be continuously portrayed as either the "hero" or the "outlaw," not simply and unbiasedly as a historical figure. This dilemma regarding Devil John is not an isolated phenomenon. The same dichotomy can be seen in works concerning the aforementioned Devil Anse Hatfield. Primarily, those who side with the Hatfields generally hold him in high regard. Conversely, many who prefer the McCoy side of the famous feud have a much different opinion.

The same historical duality can also be a matter of perspective. A good example of this would be the infamous lawman Wyatt Earp. Was he one of the "good guys" or was he a villain? Was he both? It all depends on which account you read or which movie you see. Like Devil John, he is both romanticized and demonized.

Like Wyatt Earp, Devil John became as much of a literary figure, as he was historical at the hands of later writers. The most notable of these being the man that introduced Devil John Wright to the world as the character Devil Judd Tolliver in one the first American novels to have sold more than one million copies. This man was the famous author, and John's close friend, John Fox Jr.

His book "The Trail of the Lonesome Pine" had sold more than two million copies by Fox's death, netting him a tidy fortune. Beyond this, five motion pictures, one Broadway play and two hit songs based on the 1908 novel resulted in furthering the careers of people like Cecil B. Demille and Henry Fonda. To this day the official state outdoor drama of Virginia, a live musical based on "The Trail of the Lonesome Pine," is performed every summer in Big Stone Gap, Va. It is the basis for a nice little tourist trade enjoyed by the small mountain hamlet.

The question should now be obvious. Why then am I, a direct descendant, proud great, great grandson, struggling author and incurable lover of history (especially Appalachian history)

Devil John Wright

His Life and Times

By

Philip Kent Church

SPIRIT HOLLOW PUBLISHING

BLACKSBURG, VIRGINIA

2013

Lovingly dedicated to these great, great, great, great grandchildren of "Devil" John Wesley Wright:

Cody, Sophia, Emma, Mahala, Bailey, Jesse Lee and John Wesley

writing this book? Do I seek riches? Do I desire acclaim as an Appalachian writing powerhouse? Perhaps I have a vendetta against my illustrious ancestor's old enemies, and wish to fire a final literary "shot" in some bygone feud? It may be worse than these. Maybe I'm up to some devious plot to make Devil John my very own, negating all of those who try to "lay claim" to his historic legacy; to "hitch my star" to his famous "wagon!"

While I feel quite sure that I just might be accused of all of these scurrilous motives by some Devil John aficionados out there (and believe me, they're out there) the answer is not as conniving as any of these. No, I'm simply writing this book to give to my kin and kith, my nephews, nieces and grandchildren something I was never able to find, but longed for since I was ten years old. I wish to present to them, and all of the descendants and devotees of Devil John, a volume of balanced, unbiased, historically correct and factually accurate, as is possible, telling of his life and times. I wish to finally fill the space within my own library, stocked with memoirs of misinformation and publications filled with contrived, false and shoddy scholarship regarding Devil John Wright, with a concise, correct and congenial, as is possible, telling of this man's legendary life.

To the extent that I might accomplish this, is the extent that a wonderful heritage might continue to be passed down to new generations curious about the very real man, and the uniquely American legend of Devil John Wright.

Philip Kent Church
Blacksburg, Virginia
August 18, 2013

Son of the Elkhorn

Establishing the borders of Kentucky and Virginia, rises Black Mountain. It is a four-thousand foot high ridge that extends for miles to the north and south. It is also the eastern flank of the Elkhorn Valley, a vast coal field formed by the ancient progress of Elkhorn Creek. The valley frames many of the towns of Letcher County, Kentucky, such as Dunham, McRoberts and Jenkins. It was here, in the Elkhorn, That John Wesley Wright was born on April 17, 1844.

Johns' grandparents, Joel M. Wright and Susannah Wright (her maiden name is lost to history) first settled at the head of Boone's Creek in what is now known as Kona, Kentucky around 1815. It was here, in the primal, deep Appalachian forests that John's father, Joel E. Wright was born in 1817. Joel E. would marry Eliza Bates, the daughter of the family's only neighbors, the John Bates family. The couple settled on a small parcel of John Bates' land.

Eventually they acquired their own land and raised their family of seven children, John being the second oldest. In the mountains, especially at this period of time, having as many children as possible was as much a matter of survival as it was anything else. The people of Appalachia were predominantly subsistence farmers. They couldn't afford hireling farmhands. Slavery, in that region of the country, was almost non-existent. Possessing little more than axe, plough, hoe and oxen, mountain farmers depended wholly on their families to perform the never-ending chores around their homesteads of rocky, sloping land and rudimentary buildings.

Their cabins were small, often with dirt floors. The large open fireplace and hearth, was the only means of heat and did double-duty as the cook-stove. The windows, if any, were little more than portholes, possessing no glass, as that was a luxury.

The interiors of these dwellings were usually one room with sparse furnishings of a table with a couple of wooden chairs or bench, a bed or beds according to the inhabitant's needs and stark shelves protruding from the un-plastered, log walls. Everything not on shelves was either packed within wooden chests, or hung from wooden pegs or deer antlers. This would include twists of herbs, beans, red pepper pods and tobacco. The latter was smoked by men and women alike in clay pipes, however, chewing was exclusively for the men. Even "young-uns" were not prevented from partaking, as tobacco was seen more as an indulgence rather than a harmful practice.

There would often be a cupboard near the hearth consisting of a few cups and dishes with spoons and knives used for eating; rarely were forks employed. Near the hearth would be a tripod or swing arm bearing a kettle, or cooking pot. This was usually joined by a cast iron skillet, a bread pan and Dutch oven. These mountain cabins were austere at best. They were cramped with low ceilings and perpetually dark. The fire place and tallow-dipped candles were almost the exclusive means of lighting, as lamp oil was often harder to acquire.

The diets of these rugged people consisted of cornmeal for bread or skillet-fried pone, and game meats like deer, squirrel, possum, raccoon and fish. They ate greens, usually wild, and beans from their gardens. They had garden grown and wild onions, called ramps, which fried up well with potatoes. They enjoyed wild berries for jam or cobblers and had apples, usually from their own small orchards, with which they made apple butter, deserts and cider. The women prepared and served the food. They would always wait until all of the men had eaten and then take their meals from what remained. Water, coffee, milk and cider were the beverages of the day, along with, of course, an occasional "dram" or two of corn whiskey.

The livestock consisted primarily of oxen, for hauling and plowing, chickens primarily for eggs, cows primarily for milk and butter and some had goats and sheep. An invaluable, and mandatory staple to the mountain farmers were hogs. These would be slaughtered, usually in the late fall, and provided meat throughout the unforgiving mountain winter. Everyone owned hunting dogs. These hounds would be as necessary for hunting as were guns and knives.

Horses were the only means of transportation, aside from walking. There were virtually no roads at this time. People, like John's family, would travel by horse trails, game tracks and creek beds. If any hauling had to be done, it was usually accomplished with wooden sleds pulled by oxen, rather than carriages and wagons driven by horses.

John would come to master horses and loved dealing with them. His horsemanship was far and beyond his contemporaries and would be a defining feature in his life. Indeed, he would eventually become world famous as a consummate horseman and trick-rider, but that's getting ahead of the story.

The wild of the Elkhorn, where John spent his childhood, was a beautiful, unmolested mountain paradise. The forests, having never been harvested or cleared, were ancient and thick, resulting in a perpetual ground-level darkness, even on the brightest of days. This conspired with the towering ridges and deep "hollers" to give the old saying that dusk always comes early and dawn always arrives late in the mountains.

The trails John traveled by, and the woods where he hunted were replete with stands of straight poplars, whitened birch, prized walnut, deep emerald beech, scarlet maple and the ever present evergreens. All of these would be colorfully decorated in the spring with the white dogwood and the brilliant, bright purple of the abundant red bud trees.

The sloping ridges he climbed were richly adorned with white blooming mountain laurel and rhododendron. All around would be lady slipper with pink, white and blue anemones, white blossoms of Queen Anne's lace and the highly treasured bloodroot. The sweet smell of honeysuckle hung heavily and continually in the summer's mountain air. The clean, clear streams where he would trap and fish were framed by generations of soft green willow trees and populated by rushes and cattails close into the banks. At night his way might be illuminated by the eerie, green glow of fox fire, tracing the edges of the trail as he was serenaded by calls of screech owls and whip-or-wills.

It's no wonder that John would grow to prefer trapping, tracking and hunting to the arduous chores he dutifully performed on the Wright farm. The unusually tall, black-haired lad, with steely, gray eyes, would adapt the skills of a woodsman and hunter to an uncanny level. Indeed, in the trials that would soon assail the young mountaineer, and vex him all thru his life, these skills would not only save him, but help him to overcome the many adversities that would later befall him. He knew how to survive, how to travel light and live off the land. He developed the ability to withstand the worst conditions of cold and hot, enabling him to stay on the trail for days. His talent as a horseman was exceeded only by his keen ability to track and hunt, where he developed the talents of an expert gun handler and deadly accurate marksman. Eventually, the latter would also make him world famous and, whether for good or ill, label him forever as a gunslinger.

Now, in the ante bellum Elkhorn, before the land would once again be called the "dark and bloody ground," before the coal boom and the railroads, John would enjoy an idyllic boyhood in a world of natural wonder and simple pleasures. He would join in the obligatory social "get-togethers" attended by all of his far-flung neighbors and "kin." Corn shucking parties, bean stringings, shooting matches and the occasional church meetings conducted by "ironsider" preachers and circuit riders, were the events of the day. He would help the men in raising barns and cabins for newlyweds or any incapable of doing it themselves. He would wrestle, play stretch and mumbly peg with the boys, and dance the old Virginia Reel with the girls. The latter being a lifelong preoccupation. As a young and older man alike, John always possessed a voracious and unabashed appetite for the ladies . . . any and all ladies. Indeed, among his peers, he would grow to be a man's man and a notorious playboy.

That being said, there is every indication that he was obedient to his elders and fiercely loyal to his family or "kin", and to John, if a person was his friend, they were likewise considered his kin. It would be an axiom of his life, for better or worse, thin or flush, he always did his utmost for his kin. This would be both a beneficial trait and, at times a curse.

John's kin were such that individual volumes could be written about them, aside from John's own story. This was especially true on his mother, Eliza's, side of the family. Her little brother was named Martin Van Buren Bates. This man was seven years John's senior. Saying that he was John's mother's "little" brother is a misnomer. John's uncle, Martin "Bud" Bates was seven feet, eleven inches tall and weighed in excess of four-hundred pounds; reportedly being husky in build, being neither thin nor fat. Martin Van Buren Bates was, literally, a giant

Height may have been a trait John shared with this exceptional man. While not reaching his giant size, John was well over six feet tall himself. Indeed, many of John's male progenies would grow in excess of six foot tall for over three generations. It should be no surprise that John's first nickname was "The Tall Sycamore of the Elkhorn!"

In this early time, in this primeval place, there was no such thing as a formal education. John, like the other children of the Elkhorn, would begin his "larnin" at the feet of his elders. The mountain folk weren't adverse to education and strived to convene small schools in their homes. Here, as season and chores allowed, the children would gather for several weeks at a time to learn the three "R's" by men in the community selected to teach. Bartering, land buying and horse trading were learned by young John by the side of Joel E. Wright, his "Pap." In this regard John had a keen mind and the commerce practices of the day would become a second nature to him.

There would come a time, much, much later in life that the abundant coal of the Elkhorn would turn to "black gold", and the mountain farmers would find their homesteads sitting atop a virtual fortune in mineral rights. John would, naturally, be at the vanguard of the region's conversion during the coal boom of the late 19th, and early 20th centuries. These coming marvels and the effect they would have, including national celebrity, could scarcely have been imagined by the teenaged mountain boy.

John spent much of his youth tending to chores. This included plowing, sowing, hoeing and harvesting crops on the Wright farm, and all these by the appropriate moon and zodiac signs. Wood cutting, log splitting and stacking cords of firewood, repairing and replacing wood-hewn shingles, running fence, (split-rails) slopping the hogs and providing corn fodder for the cattle would all be in a day's work for the muscular young man. By seventeen, he'd lived a life of unparalleled beauty and hardship. In this wholesome, mountain environment he grew and thrived, life could not have been more ideal.

Sadly, however, a war was coming to Kentucky. It would be the crucible wherein the guileless, young woodsman of the Elkhorn would become an adept killer of men. It was 1861. John was seventeen. His ingenuous youth in the Elkhorn was over, and nothing, absolutely nothing, would ever be the same!

It is at this point in the narrative that a pause must occur. The problem is one of simple mathematics, but the effect upon the text is huge.

John is about to enter the Civil War. The war began on April 12, 1861. John's tombstone has his birth recorded as April 17th, 1844, seventeen years earlier. However, John is denoted by virtually all newspaper articles, genealogies and family histories as joining the 13th Kentucky Calvary on July 4th, 1862. These all state that he joined the war prior to his seventeenth birthday. Now, if you do the math, at enlistment, John would've actually been eighteen years old not, as is generally held, sixteen years old at enlistment.

Compounding this is the fact that many of the aforementioned publications, including, his son, W. T. Wright's book and Epling's book, give John's birth date as April 17th, 1842. This is a full two years earlier than what is inscribed on the man's tombstone, causing his enlistment age to have been twenty years old. John's brother, Solomon actually was born in 1842 and the two may simply have been confused, one with the other. Further compounding this is the fact that the 13th Kentucky Cavalry was known by John himself as the 10th Kentucky Cavalry or 10th Kentucky Mounted Infantry or Rifles.

Lastly, while all the publications regarding his enlistment as occurring July 4th 1862, with some stating it was July 4th 1861, (making him over 17 at enlistment) the official records, the actual roster of the 13th Kentucky Cavalry, show that Private John Wright enlisted October 4th 1862 at Whitesburg, Kentucky --- on the same day Thomas Talton Hall was also enlisted. This man would later be known as "Bad" Talt Hall, "The Terror of the Cumberlands." He would also become John Wright's closest friend. Unfortunately, throughout their lives in the popular mind and press, the two were continually being confused with each other.

Talt was two years younger than John. He was born in 1846 and actually was sixteen years old when he enlisted alongside John. It is, perhaps, this fact being erroneously attributed to John Wright that explains the historical discrepancy regarding John's age at enlistment.

It is this date, October 4th, 1862, that a good historian must follow, as well as the inscribed birth date on his headstone. This means that John Wesley Wright was over eighteen years old (18 years, 2 months, 17 days to be exact) when he was inducted into the Confederate Army.

That being said, there does exist the remote possibility that he could've been mustered into the 10th Calvary on Independence Day, 1861 while seventeen years old and the records were changed when the 10th became the 13th Kentucky Calvary. At this point such a contention is so dubious, it must be ignored, the October 4th, 1862 date remains the best conclusion. It is an unfortunate fact that dependable birth records for mountaineers in the 19th century, as well as Confederate Army records in general, are somewhat lacking. Researchers and historians are bound to do the best they can for the veracity of their publications, committing to the best preserved, best documented and most sensible source material for their conclusions.

The Fog of War

The Civil War broke-out in 1861 after decades of argument, political dissension and an ever widening chasm of public opinion on one issue . . . slavery. However, the basic, driving forces were, threefold - a "cause," which was state rights vs. federal power - a "reason," which, as stated, was slavery, and a "compulsion," which was economic survival (some would say "greed").

The frontier spirit and its love of liberty, born in the original colonies, now spearheaded the Western expansion of the United States. This resulted in the opening of territories that would eventually become states themselves. This included Missouri, Louisiana, Kansas, Nebraska and Texas.

Well-heeled Southerners, needing to expand their agriculturally based economy, wanted to move into these new territories and transport their privately owned property with them. This included their slaves, which were considered to be, more or less, merely "livestock." It was, for their way of life, a matter of nothing less than sheer survival. The vast Southern farming operations were exhausting the land. Laws enacted earlier in the 19th century had severely restricted the slave trade, and the price of new slaves had super-inflated.

To break new ground for farming, and raise new, free labor to do all of the work, they had to be able to settle these new territories and take what they perceived as their "property" with them. The North, with the newly formed, anti-slavery, Republican Party led by Abraham Lincoln, was having none of it.

The North was highly industrialized and urbanized. It depended very little upon the human bondage that was American slavery. As a result, the North sought a policy of containment regarding the new territories, forbidding the practice of slavery from growing thru expansion. The belief was that, if restricted to the Southern states, slavery would inexorably die out.

With this the impasse was set. The subsequent election of a Republican, the aforementioned Abraham Lincoln, to President was the last straw   Eleven Southern states would quickly secede from the twenty-five states of the Union, and form the Confederate States of America. On April 12th, 1861, little more than one month after Lincoln's inauguration, the federal installation at Fort Sumter, in South Carolina, was attacked and captured by the newly formed Confederacy. The bloodiest war in American history had begun

At the beginning of the war John's home state of Kentucky was officially neutral. Unofficially, a Confederate state government was formed, but in exile. By the war's end, Kentucky would officially ally itself with the Union, and join the Northern states in the fray.

Their neighbor to the east, however, was a defining part of the Confederacy. Virginia, rather than follow Lincoln's call for volunteer troops to fight against the Confederacy, would join their Southern neighbors and, actually, become the deciding state in the war   The capitol of the Confederate states would be located in Richmond, Virginia. Indeed, it would be in the "Old

Dominion" that "Dixie" would finally surrender . . . and fall.

John Wright's home in the Elkhorn formed Kentucky's border with this vital Confederate state. As in the rest of the border-states, the Appalachian citizenry was divided between those who aligned with the North, called "Unionists", and those who believed in the South, known as the "Rebels."

Of the three, previously stated, motivations for the war, which of these would cause many, if not most, of the Kentucky mountain folk to side with the Confederacy? Was the motivation an economic one? The answer is no. Mountaineers were predominantly subsistence farmers. There were no large plantations, to speak of, in Appalachia. There was no remarkable farming of cotton. The issues of the economic survival of the South simply didn't apply to the Appalachian regions of eastern Kentucky, Southwestern Virginia and Eastern Tennessee.

Was protecting and expanding the practice of slavery a prime motivator? The answer has to be, absolutely not. For all practical purposes, slavery, in Appalachia, simply did not exist. The mountaineers, being isolated during western expansion from the urbanization, agricultural and industrial progress of the rest of the country, vigorously retained their frontier spirit of self-reliance. They were fierce adherents to the notions of a strong work ethic and independence. Plainly stated, while not being adverse to slavery as an institution, the idea of forcing another to do chores that could be done by oneself would've probably been regarded as a type of laziness. In spite of the "hillbilly" stereotype, the inhabitants of the mountains were abhorrent of being, and anything but, 'lazy!' Along with this, they were basically too poor to afford slavery, even if they wanted it. When it comes to the slavery issue, Appalachia simply didn't have a "dog in that fight."

This leaves the issue of the rights of the states vs. the authority of the federal government. This, particularly in regard to the disposition of private property owned by the citizens of a particular state, and the liberty to transplant that property between states and territories. Repugnant as it is to modern sensibilities, and rightfully so, the "property" in question was people. These were human beings that were, both socially and legally, regarded as mere property --- the slaves.

In the mind-set of the time, the federal government had no more right to tell a citizen what they could do with their slaves than they did their horses, cattle and pigs. The ill-conceived belief was that such encroachment upon legally held property was nothing less than an exercise of tyranny by the government in Washington, being perpetuated upon the law-abiding citizens of sovereign states. Of course, the ugly truth was that without slavery, and the ability to expand it, fortunes, and opulent, "white," Southern lifestyles would be forever "gone with the wind!"

It is this perceived tyranny by the federal government upon the liberties of citizens in self-governing states that likely repulsed the rugged individualists of the Appalachians. To resist and rebel against such tyranny targeting one's homeland and personal rights seemed, at the time, a laudable, and celebrated endeavor. It was actually a misconstrued loyalty to liberty itself that resounds to this very day in one phrase . . . "Southern Pride!"

It may be asked. Being a product of this society, how racist was John Wright? Was he the stereotypical "Southern man" who hated African-Americans to the extent that he would risk his own life in a war to ensure their oppression? Based on the historical record, the answer seems to be a surprising, no.

Consider the following. There are photographs of John riding side by side with African-Americans. In the book, "Devil John Wright of the Cumberlands" his son, W. T. Wright, relates how John worked in the field alongside an African-American.

Not wishing to jump too far ahead, it must be noted that John began the war as a Confederate, but finished as a Union soldier. Whatever the reasons (to be addressed later) along the way he had a change of heart, and finished on the winning side of the war, and of history. Lastly, and perhaps, most tellingly, at the century's end lawman "Devil" John Wright led a two year war of attrition that utterly destroyed the K.K.K. in Letcher County, Kentucky!

Did he view African-Americans as being equal? Assuredly, his upbringing in the 19th century South would've probably precluded this. However, it should be remembered that, due to a well-earned arrogance, he would not have seen any man as his equal, regardless of color or stripe. While it remains certain that he held prejudices instilled by his environment, he does seem to have been somewhat ahead of his time in regard to race.

Why did John Wright join the war? The answer seems to be a healthy wanderlust combined with the, previously mentioned, notion of "Southern Pride". In an article published just after his death in the Mountain Eagle newspaper, Letcher County, Kentucky, John is quoted as saying; *"I was fully determined to do my best for my sunny southland, and have never regretted it."* He was obviously motivated by a sense of defending his homeland, and protecting his heritage.

Here is another article which appeared in The Mountain Eagle newspaper, Letcher County, Kentucky, on February 5th 1931. It is a memorial article written by a Mr. Webb, the paper's editor. Here, John is relating his war experiences.

"You have heard me tell of my hard life in the war. You know that the battles in the Valleys of Virginia were enough to chill and deaden the heart of a grown man, but we were boys, and there was a number of us from Letcher County stood up to the task like men, and some of us lived to get back to home and mother. You have read of the battle of Old Shilo. All day on that dreadful Sunday, often in water and mud up to our hips, we struggled and fought and died. The picture of that awful struggle will never fade from my memory. I saw hundreds of fair-faced, blue eyed boys, the sons of some praying mothers, swept into the crimson mud and water never to come out. If carnage like that wouldn't harden men's souls what would? General Albert Sydney Johnston was killed that day and it was an awful blow to the Confederate cause."

In this interview John is giving an accurate description of the Battle of Shiloh, Tennessee. Here's the problem. The famous battle occurred April 6 - 7th, 1862. This is almost five months before John's recorded enlistment date of October 4th of the same year!

It appears that one of three things may be happening here. John, like so many old war veterans, is simply embellishing his experiences during the war, and was never at Shiloh. Secondly, Mr. Webb is fleshing-out John's story to help his article, or sell papers, or both. Or lastly, John, like untold numbers of young men of the time, had just shown-up and volunteered to fight for the Confederate Army, ending up at Shiloh. After this he might've returned to Kentucky and officially enlisted that following fall. He may, indeed, have fought at Shiloh. If the latter is the most accurate, this would be the first combat involving John Wright on record. As such, it has been, cautiously, included here.

The Battle of Shiloh

Shiloh is a Hebrew word that, ironically, means "peace". It is also the name for an old church near the banks of the Tennessee River. It was here on April 6th, 1862 that the Army of Tennessee for the Union, under command of Maj. Gen. Ulysses S. Grant, had made camp. They were awaiting the Army of the Ohio, under command of Maj. Gen. D. C. Buell, to join them for an ongoing campaign in the Western Theater.

Gen. Sydney Albert Johnston, commanding The Army of Mississippi for the Confederacy, ordered a surprise attack on the Union forces at Shiloh. He was wishing to defeat Grant's army before they could be reinforced by Buell. At first, the battle was dominated by the Rebels and looked like a Confederate victory. Unfortunately, the Confederate ranks became confused and the army was in disarray. Then, Gen. Johnston was killed. He would have the dubious distinction of being the highest ranking officer to be killed in the entire war. His second in command, Gen. P. G. T. Beauregard, ordered a full retreat as darkness fell. That was a mistake!

That night The Army of the Ohio finally reached Shiloh, swelling the Union forces to almost seventy-thousand men. The combined forces struck a counterattack at dawn. The result was a catastrophic defeat for the Confederates, and the bloodiest battle of the war to date. Close to twenty-four thousand casualties would be counted, including almost thirty-five hundred killed.

The Battle of Gladeville

July 6th 1863, Private John W. Wright is standing his post at Gladeville (later renamed Wise), Virginia, just a few miles east of the Kentucky border. The tall nineteen year old, with a shock of thick, black hair and gray eyes that matched his uniform, had been mustered in the small town along with the 13th Kentucky Cavalry, under the command of Col. Ben Caudill. That night his commanders were carousing at "balls" throughout the village. Meanwhile, a unit of Union soldiers out of Ohio was, stealthily, making its way outside the town's limits.

The next day, July 7th, the town was attacked. Though caught unprepared the Confederate soldiers, along with members of the town's volunteer "Home Guard," fought valiantly. This would be to no avail. John and his comrades were forced to retreat and hole-up in the county courthouse. The Union soldiers surrounded them and they were given a choice. The defenders could surrender and the building be spared, or they'd be burned alive and the courthouse destroyed. To the consternation of the Confederates, especially young John, they were forced to surrender. What happened next is revealed in the following excerpt. This is based on an interview with a man whose grandfather was one of John's compatriots that day. This is taken from the book, "The Mountain, The Miner and the lord: and Other Tales from a Country law Office", by Harry M. Caudill.

> *"The Confederates came out with their hands high, their little fortress ringed by bayonets. A Yankee captain advanced to meet them, his fingers grasping the reins of a splendid black horse. Private Wright was at the rear of the vanquished confederates. Suddenly he yanked a concealed pistol out of his shirt and rushed forward, shot the unfortunate captain in the face, and leaped onto his saddle. Bending low, he spurred the horse and rushed away amid a hail of misdirected bullets. The perfidious murder of their captain aroused the wrath of the Union soldiers and they came "within a hair" of killing my grandfather and the rest of the Rebel soldiers then and there."*

That day ninety-seven regular troops and twenty-three officers, including Col. Caudill, were captured. Obviously, John wasn't among them. The young Rebel had employed the incomparable talents of marksmanship and horsemanship, he'd gained growing-up in the Elkhorn, to effect his daring escape. It's precisely these two skills that would be hallmarks of John Wright's life.

While John is described as displaying an impressive courage in his escape, this excerpt may be even more revealing. The use of the word "perfidious" on the part of the narrator might be telling in this respect. Perfidious basically means treacherous. Undoubtedly it's employed here to address the way John double-crossed his Union captors. It might also be applied to John's comrades.

It seems that John did what he did with little concern for the way it would affect his fellow prisoners. As he would do throughout his life, he was looking out for "number one." He saw the opportunity to live to fight another day and, perhaps, steal a "splendid black horse" in the bargain. Beyond these, it is possible that nothing else entered into his calculus. Indeed, the passage goes on to relate how terribly John's companions were treated as a result of his actions. That being the case, it must be noted that these same men applauded what he did as delivering a "black-eye" to their captors.

For more than a year following his escape at Gladeville, John's war experiences become a little cloudy. The source materials have him being somewhat of a mercenary, offering his services to more than a few Confederate causes in different battle fronts of the war. Some sources, including W. T. Wright's book, have John acting as a spy and courier operating between Abingdon, Virginia and Cynthiana, Kentucky. As to this, no specific stories seem to exist. However, possessing his extraordinary capabilities as a horseman and woodsman, such an undertaking would've been a natural choice for him.

He is said to have been at Fort Smith, Arkansas where it's thought that he was captured, but, once again, escaped. As in the previous case, no confirmable specifics seem to exist. What is generally agreed on is that, by 1864, he is found to be in Tennessee (perhaps Blountsville) under the command of the infamous Brig. Gen. John Hunt Morgan.

Was John Wright one of "Morgan's Raiders?" The answer depends on precisely what is defined by the term. If by this it's meant, was John one of the, close to, twenty-five hundred Confederates that participated in the illustrious, three state raid led by Gen. Morgan from June 11th to July 26th, 1863? The answer has to be, no. As covered previously, John was hundreds of miles away with the 13th Kentucky Cavalry at Gladeville, Virginia while the excursion known as "Morgan's Raid" was occurring.

Was John involved in subsequent "raids" conducted under Gen. Morgan's command? The answer is a confirmed, yes. In this respect he was, in truth, one of "Morgan's Raiders." This has caused more than a little confusion, but there can be no other conclusion. He served under Morgan, and he was a raider. Thus Pvt. John W. Wright may be considered one of "Morgan's Raiders."

The Battle of Cynthiana

On June 6th, 1864, Gen. Morgan attacked the Union held town of Cynthiana in Harrison County, Kentucky. Among the approximate twelve-hundred Confederate cavalrymen was John Wright. As at Shiloh, the first day of the battle went well for the Confederates. The second day they were routed by an overwhelming Union force. Almost all of Morgan's men were either captured, killed or wounded. Among the latter was John!

The twenty year old had received multiple wounds in the abdomen and thighs. Avoiding capture, he crawled an estimated two-hundred yards to obtain cover underneath some foliage by a creek. This event would, forever, change the young man's life

 A Harrison County farmer named Jamisson Humphrey found the wounded Confederate. The man hid John in his wagon, and took him to his home. There John met Jamisson's twenty-seven year old daughter, Martha Humphrey. John called her "Mattie."

For the next few weeks the Humphreys took care of John, hiding him from the Union soldiers and Cynthiana Home Guard. It would fall to Mattie to tend to John's wounds. Evidently this drew the couple intimately close. As much as he could for anyone alive, it appears that John fell in love with this belle of the Bluegrass. That being the case, his wounds adequately healed, John returned to his unit in faraway Tennessee. Nine months later, on May 23, 1865, the unmarried Mattie gave birth to John's first son, James

Of Gray and Blue

The next year of John's life is obscured by the "fog of war." As best as can be ascertained, it appears that, during a subsequent raid into Kentucky, Pvt. John Wright is, once again, captured. There are reports that he was first held in close-by Lexington, Kentucky, this is the most likely. Other sources have him being transported, once again, to faraway Fort Smith, Arkansas.

In spite of this, it is known that he, eventually, was sent to Columbus, Ohio, possibly to the same federal prison which held his Confederate comrades captured during Morgan's Raid. After swearing his allegiance to the Union, and promising to remain north of the Ohio River, John Wright was released. Whether this change of heart was based on a rethinking of his personal politics, or due to the fact that the
Confederacy was heading towards an obvious defeat, or was John, as always, looking out for number one, and being given little choice in the matter, is not known. Leaving prison, the young expatriate headed east toward West Virginia.

During the Civil War the federal government had issued a draft. A provision of the law allowed for a drafted person to be substituted by another, especially if a "commutation" fee was paid. Thus, families who could afford the commutation money could prevent their young male relatives from being forced to serve, by paying someone else to enlist in their stead.
It was just such a family, their identity is unknown, that John happened upon in Eastern Ohio. Receiving a reported three-hundred dollar fee to enlist instead of a drafted family member, John Wright actually rejoined the war . . . as a Union soldier. It was 1865. What is interesting is that, rather than breaking his bond and absconding with the money, John followed thru and donned the blue uniform of the enemy he'd been fighting for the previous three years. Whether or not he saw combat as a union soldier is not clear. Be that as it may, as previously stated, he finished on the winning side of the war, and history.

On April 9th of that same year, Confederate Gen. Robert E. Lee surrendered to Union Gen. Ulysses S. Grant at Appomattox Courthouse, Virginia. Within two months the last shots would be fired. It was June, 1865 . . . the Civil War was over.

The Giant, The Wife and The Circus of Life

The war was over, but the damage done to the people of the mountains was profound and irrevocable. With the vast amount of fathers, sons and brothers away fighting the war, the region had descended into destitution and lawlessness. Poverty was rampant and outlaws, both Unionists and Rebels, had turned into gangs of marauders unleashed upon the austere population which remained in the "hills." The Appalachian society that war veterans discovered after returning home was fractured into clannish factions protecting what little property and provisions they had left. Now, in the post-war mountains, just as slaughter follows harvest, vengeance would follow violence. The era of the "mountain feuds" had begun in earnest

It was late spring, 1865 when twenty-one year old John Wright returned to the Elkhorn. Joel E. Wright, his father, now forty-eight, had to be convinced that John was who he claimed to be. Joel had heard that his second oldest son had been killed in 1863 near Fort Smith, Arkansas. This, along with the changes in John's appearance, affected by three years of war, caused Joel to not initially recognize his own son

John found a region, a society and kinfolk ravaged by the war. The wounds were fresh and deep. The Wright farm was in disarray. His neighbors lived in fear and distrust of each other. The depravity and violence of the day had hardened the hearts and souls of the remaining populace. Life had become cheap. John discovered that his older brother, Solomon, had been brutally murdered and one of his uncles, on his mother's side, had been gruesomely tortured to death during his absence. For the killers of these men, these were huge mistakes!

In 1863 Solomon, John's eldest brother, was forced to steal food for himself and his 'woman' in Lee County, Virginia. The owner of the spring house Solomon pilfered tracked him to his home. Along with two other men, including a man named Irving Hill from Gunter, Tennessee, they killed the couple in cold blood for Solomon's petty crime. Irving Hill was the one who killed Solomon.

During the war John's Uncle Bates had been abducted by eight unionists. The group mercilessly tortured the hapless man to a slow and grisly death with their bayonets. These marauders could not have conceivably picked a worse person to victimize, if they'd tried. This was not so much that they had brutally murdered the uncle of John Wright; no, they had killed the older, beloved brother of seven foot, eleven inch tall, four-hundred twenty-five pound Martin Van Buren Bates, purported to be the largest man on record at the time . . . in the world! As stated, this was a huge mistake!

Martin Bates would become world famous as the "Kentucky Giant," but preferred to be called "Captain" Bates. This was due to his reported rank upon leaving the Confederate Army, though his headstone records he was a First Lieutenant. The giant donned his Confederate uniform along with his specially made sword which was a full foot and a half longer than the standard issue. He strapped on his .71 caliber "horse" pistols, mounted his oversized Percheron horse he'd acquired in Pennsylvania, and set upon his terrible vendetta against his brother's murderers.

Bates was joined by other mountaineers and kin, including Joel E. And, of course, his son, John Wright. After a time these men had captured, not only, the eight accused, but their entire families, including their children. The giant's "posse" led this group to a popular crossroads in Letcher County. At first light the doomed men and their pleading families beheld a crudely built gallows constructed between two oak trees containing eight nooses. The gallows had been specifically designed to ensure the slow strangulation of its victims rather than quickly snapping their necks.

At the sun's dawning above the tall ridges, the giant, mounted on his tall horse, raised his mighty sword, and gave the signal for the limb, the noosed men were precariously balancing on, to be kicked away. As their fathers, wives, mothers, sons and daughters watched in horror, the wretched victims kicked at the air for over a half an hour.

Still, the giant's rage was not satiated by the men's death. Before releasing the families, the giant proclaimed that the bodies must not ever be taken down, but would remain as a warning to anyone who'd be foolish enough to kill a Bates. The punishment for tending to their dead kin would be a similar fate, and their farms and homes would be razed. Then, and only then, it was over. The Kentucky Giant had his vengeance. With little more than rumor and innuendo to convict them, "mountain justice" had been delivered upon the eight individuals who, for all is known, could've actually been partially or wholly innocent of the crime. As stated, life, in the post-war Elkhorn, had become "cheap."

Now, it was twenty-one year old John Wright's turn for mountain justice upon the man who'd cold-bloodedly murdered his brother, Solomon. John first traveled to Lee County, Virginia where he investigated the crime. He learned the killer's name and residence in Gunter, Tennessee. The young horseman, and expert marksman, set out to the south and Tennessee to fulfill his retribution upon Irving Hill. Upon arriving in Gunter, John found out that Hill was seated, along with five others, upon a fence
between the general store and the town's post office. The six men were simply whiling away the afternoon with whittling, chewing "baccer" and spinning yarns when John Wright rode up to them. What happened next is related by W. T. Wright in his book "Devil John Wright of the Cumberlands".

"He inquired for Mr. Irivin Hill and a tall raw-boned man answered to the name.At the answer John pulled his pistol and shot three times before the man fell from the fence.

"Boys," he said, "This man came to my home and killed my brother. Now they are even. Do any of you want to take up the quarrel?" They were silent and John swung his horse around and started to return home."

John had avenged his brother's death employing the same, pragmatic form of mountain justice used by his giant uncle. Moreover, John had utilized his keen investigatory skills along with the abilities he possessed as a woodsman, horseman and gunman. This was the first use of a skill-set, pursuing an outlaw, which he enjoyed, was very good at and would serve him well in the years to come as a bona fide lawman. However, for the time being, the handsome young veteran had other things on his mind.

John returned to Letcher and took up with a lovely, twenty-two year old mountain girl named Margaret Austin. He also found favor with Margaret's seven year older sister Surrilda (some places her name is listed as Serilda). The problem was, he got them both pregnant, at the same time! This doesn't seem to have been a "bone of contention" between the Austin sisters. Indeed, Surrilda would name her daughter, fathered by John, "Margaret", after her sister. Around the same time, in the winter of 1866, Margaret gave birth to her daughter by John and named her Mahala, a Creek Indian word meaning "beautiful". By the time of these births, while allowing his surname, Wright, to be given to the children (as he would do with all of his children, all thirty-three of them) John would leave the region.

As the months rolled into the summer of 1866 the Kentucky Giant relented on his order concerning the, now skeletonized, remains of the eight men he lynched. He allowed them to be removed for burial. He also became convinced that the children he forced to watch the executions would grow-up and, sooner or later, come calling for their vengeance upon him. To avoid the inevitable scythe of mountain justice from swinging his way, he prudently decided to leave the area. John, his favorite nephew, would join him in a secret journey to the west. The giant would leave his nephew and travel from the Bluegrass to Cincinnati. John, however, headed on to Cynthiana to join his firstborn son, one year old James, and the woman he'd fallen in love with during the war --- Mattie Humphrey.

On October 14th, 1866, at the Humphrey farm, John legally married the twenty-nine year old Mattie, described as being a vivacious woman with red apple colored hair.
It's reported that John settled on the Humphrey farm with his new wife and son. He blended in with the other citizens of Cynthiana, and seemed to do well.

The Bluegrass section of Kentucky was, and still is, famous for the breeding and racing of horses. Even Edgar Cacey, the famous "sleeping prophet" of Hopkinsville, Kentucky, lamented that he was continually asked to use his "gift" to reveal which horse would win in a given race. Horses were a big business. The stealing of a prized Bluegrass racehorse was the worst type of crime that one could commit, ranking with murder. Regardless, a man committed the unthinkable, stole such a prized horse from a
Cynthiana breeder and escaped upon his ill-gotten booty. A posse was immediately formed and set out in search of the thief. Joining these men was John Wright.

The posse tracked the thief northward to the bank of the Ohio River. The men tried to figure out if their quarry had traveled up or downstream, or worse, had somehow doubled back and escaped. However, John reckoned that the thief had actually forced his mount to swim the mighty river to the Ohio side. Furthermore, he reasoned that if a horse-thief could do it, so could he!

The Ohio at its most narrow could not have been any less than well over a hundred yards wide, if that. The current is a strong west/southwest one and the depth is always at least forty feet. As such, it remains to this day a major inland waterway. The idea of such a span being crossed on horseback was an incredulous one which none of the posse wanted to attempt. That is, none but the young mountaineer from Letcher County.

John prepared his horse and himself, bid his companions farewell then spurred his mount into the deep water. Several tedious minutes later, the remaining men beheld their intrepid young comrade emerge onto the far bank on the Ohio side It may be asked, is such a feat possible? Could a man guide a horse to swim across the Ohio River without drowning the poor beast? According to the veterinarians at Appalachian Veterinarian Services in Christiansburg, Virginia, renowned for their equestrian expertise, the answer is an unbelievable . . . yes!

After a while, John regained the thief's track, and continued the hunt by himself. Within a couple of days he found the man, still riding the stolen horse. John shot and killed the man, and some days later returned with the prized animal. John claimed he killed the man in self-defense. Whether his assertion was true or not no one knew, nor, because the victim was a no-good horse-thief, cared. The end justified whatever means John Wright employed in the horse's recovery!

After this, before the end of 1866, whether by invitation or inclination, John left his wife and son at the family farm and rejoined his giant uncle in Cincinnati. "Captain" Bates had been exhibiting his colossal frame, billed as "The Mountain Giant," at the famous "Governor" John Robinson Circus which had a permanent venue at Fifth and Vine in downtown Cincinnati.

The Robinson Circus had been started by "Governor's" father and had made its base of operations in Cincinnati since 1856. After surviving a riot in 1861 at Lexington, Kentucky for flying the "stars and stripes," rather than the "stars and bars," the circus refused to perform below the Ohio River.

Governor had received his nickname while training as a trick-rider when he was a boy. The show's billed trick-rider, who trained the young lad, was from England. The man's horse groom, also from England, called young John Robinson, Governor ("Guv-nah") Robinson. The name stuck to remain with him all of his life.

During the Civil War, Governor enlisted with the Union and was detailed to a gunboat on the Mississippi. It's reported that he victoriously fought many battles on the Mississippi, including the Battle of Vicksburg. In 1865, at the age of twenty-three, Governor was discharged and returned to the circus, as its proprietor. During his time as "ringmaster" the Robinson Circus would grow to be rivaled only by the P. T. Barnum show. Indeed, the most famous clown in the world, Emmett Kelly Jr.'s father, Emmet Kelly Sr., would receive his start in the Robinson "Ring!"

Now, young John Wright would join his illustrious uncle in the show. While Martin Bates headlined as "The Mountain Giant," John, presumably under the tutelage of Governor, would become a trick-rider   Along with this, based on his extraordinary talents with a gun, John added some trick-shooting to the act.

Aside from the obligatory acrobatics of leaping from saddle to tail, and back to saddle, performing handstands and bouncing from one side of the horse to the other. John would duck underneath the horse's neck and bulls-eye a target at full gallop. Reportedly he could empty his pistol in this fashion, firing all shots in rapid succession, never missing his mark   This was to the delight of the crowds watching his performance.

John's favorite gun was a converted Navy Colt .44 caliber that he claimed he took from a dead soldier during the war, and called his "war gun." He would prefer this weapon to all others throughout his entire life, and kept it in pristine condition. While it's hopeful that this gun still exists, its trail grows cold with the death of John's son, Frank Wright, in the 1970's. However, photographs of the famous firearm, titled "The Law of the Hills," can still be found in published works and online. While newspaper reports of the day state that the grip of the infamous weapon contained no less than twenty-eight notches, the photos reveal that this wasn't so. Besides this, it is highly doubtful that John would've defaced his favorite pistol in any way . . . regardless of how many men he'd actually killed with it.

John, along with his uncle, would perform and tour with the circus for, at least, two years. Not only did this encompass the United States, but England and Europe as well. Admittedly there remains contention as to whether or not John actually crossed the Atlantic with the show. It remains as likely to be true as not. What is proven to be myth is the long held assertion that John performed before Queen Victoria in 1870. The Queen was reportedly so impressed with the circus that she presented the Mountain Giant with a giant-sized pocket watch as a token of her esteem

The truth is that John had left the circus by 1868, but his uncle stayed on. In London, England, Martin Bates married Anna Swan, eight foot tall Anna Swan, from Nova Scotia. The union made them the tallest couple in the world, a record held until the 1960's!   This conspicuous marriage so delighted Queen Victoria that she may have attended the wedding, in person. This occurred, not in 1870 but, in 1874, when the Queen presented the royally commissioned, oversized pocket watch to the giant groom as a wedding gift --- John Wright simply was not there.

It appears that John bid the circus life farewell in the spring of 1868. He returned to the Humphrey farm in Cynthiana, gathered up his wife and child, and moved back to the Elkhorn. Mattie, his wife, would never see the Bluegrass again. She was thirty-one and John was twenty-four at the time.

The small family settled-in to the rustic life of the Kentucky Mountains. Mattie assumed the duties of her role, keeping house, tending to the garden and whatever chickens, cows and other livestock they owned.

About the same time, John started visiting Surrilda, the older of the Austin sisters, again. This resulted in the subsequent, 1869, birth of his second son, Enoch Wright.

This was also the second child he fathered with Surrilda. Whether or not Mattie knew about this, or cared, is not known. Suffice it to say that such indiscretions by married men of the time were quite common. Many wives adopted the attitude that it didn't matter who their husbands were out with, or what they did with their time, as long as they knew who to come home to. Whether this was Mattie's philosophy or not is simply not known.

What is clear is that John would eventually father thirty more children by five other women beyond the one he was legally married to. Without exception the children would all bear his surname, and the women were all referred to as "wives."

Devil John
Lawman

For approximately forty years, from around 1870 to 1910, John Wright worked as a "lawman" in various capacities. He originally did this in an unofficial manner wherein he simply came to the aid of his neighbors and community.

The Appalachian region was virtually lawless after the Civil war. The railroads and coal companies had not yet brought "civilization" to the "hills." American expansion had somewhat overshot the mountains of Appalachia in its "manifest destiny" toward the Wild West. Indeed, there was probably a better social structure and rule of law in the Old West than existed in the isolated mountain communities of deep Appalachia in the late 19th, early 20th centuries.

It can be said that, at times, John Wright took the law into his own hands. The point is well taken, but what other choice was there? Some men of good will and strong notions of right and wrong, like John, had to step-up to ensure the "peace" of the community against the wholesale lawlessness that existed after the war. It took men who were fearless and, admittedly, lived by the "feud" to stand in the gap!

The notion of due process, inasmuch as accused outlaws were concerned, barely existed in this time and place. It was more common for the doctrines of victims' rights and citizen's arrests to be employed than the precepts of probable cause and rights of the accused, in stemming the ever rising tide of crime. Simply put, if justice was to be had by the mountaineers, they had to do it, like so many other things in their lives, themselves.

This was a time when wanted men would show up to court with their "kin," usually drunk and always heavily armed. More than a few courts were "shot-up," and more than a few judges and prosecutors were held at gunpoint as the outlaws simply did what they wanted on the days their cases were on the docket. It was in the capacity of ensuring the safety of courts that John Wright was first employed. Against such criminals John, sometimes alone and sometimes with his own "kin," was first engaged to allow the court's business to go forward.

One such episode is related by John's son, W. T. Wright in his memoir, "Devil John Wright of the Cumberlands." Here the author tells that a man named "Captain" Jack Combs and a band of eleven of his kin had been holding up the court at Hazard, Kentucky. Elicited for his help by the judge, John Wright and six of his kin laid in wait the day court came back into session. On schedule, drunk and armed, Captain Jack and his men seated themselves on the front row of the courtroom. When the case of Jack's kinsman was called, the twelve men rose to their feet and pulled their guns on the judge and prosecutor. As this happened, John Wright and his men stealthily entered the courtroom. John's men positioned themselves directly behind the row of Jack's men, and drew their weapons. The following excerpt reveals what happened next.

"the argument began to intensify, but they had not seen what was taking place in the back of them. ...

No sooner had the captain finished his idle boast than a cool, calm, but resolute command met his ear.

"Captain, you're covered and every man you got. Drop that gun and stick up your hands every man of you." . . . We're going to have court here today if we have to kill Jack Combs and every man in his gang."

Understandably, the men gave up their weapons! Presumably court was held, but at the judge's behest Captain Jack and his men were taken into custody by John. They were subsequently transported to Jackson, Kentucky to be tried for their crimes in a different county with no further interference. This time, as in many instances, a court was able to operate with the help of John Wright.

It should be noted that the previous story took place in Perry County not Letcher. Such was John Wright's reputation that his services were employed throughout the mountainous counties of Eastern Kentucky. It is reported that often his mere presence, alone, in a particular court was enough to check any unlawful interruptions!

John's reputation was not only confined to those who upheld the law, but those who, regarding themselves in political defiance, broke the law. Such was the case of the infamous Jesse James!

In the book "The Mountain, the Miner, and the Lord and Other Tales from a Country Law Office," Harry M. Caudill relates that, according to John's nephew, Tilden Wright, John Wright and some of his kin ("gang") escorted Jesse James and his gang from Ohio through Eastern Kentucky to Cumberland Gap, to effect the James Gang's safe passage to Tennessee. Reportedly John was given twenty-two thousand dollars by Jesse himself as payment to John and his men for guiding and guarding him from any who wished to capture the famous outlaw. Apparently, during the arduous trek the two men, John and Jesse, got along quite well, and held each other in high esteem. Consider the following excerpt from Caudill's book. It is an interview conducted with Mattie Wright Houston, one of John's granddaughters, after his death.

"Grandpap had a lot of guns and one day he undertook to clean and oil them. . . .

"Finally he come to a pistol with pretty pearl handles and I said, "grandpap, where did you get that one?" He picked it up and looked at it, and thought a little while before he answered. "Honey, Jesse James gave me that pistol. I did him a great favor once and he seemed to appreciate it a mighty lot. When I left him he said, here, Wright, this is for you - a gift from Jesse James!"

Aside from his duties as a "guardian" for such notables as Jesse James and the courts of the region, John was eventually employed in more official capacities. It is presumed by the historical record that sometime between the mid 1870's and 1885 John was enlisted as a Deputy

Sheriff of Letcher County, and later installed as Magistrate

Regardless, John's career as a deputy has been passed down in the form of a handful of undated stories wherein his reputation as a fearless lawman, and relentless man-hunter is always mentioned. It was the first aspect of his courage when dealing with the numerous criminals, bushwhackers and outlaws populating the post-war Elkhorn, which earned him the title of "Bad" John. It would be the latter trait of his relentlessness in tracking down those he held warrants for, that earned him the title he's most renowned for. Sometime during the late 1870's he would earn, as a Letcher County lawman, the indelible name of "Devil" John Wright The universal assertion is that this dubious moniker came from the men he hunted down and brought to justice. It was said that to have "Bad" John on your trail was "like having the devil at your heels!" Thus "Devil" John Wright was born!

There have been some detractors of this who claim that "Bad" John wasn't referred to as "Devil" John until after the 1908 publication of John Fox Jr.'s novel, "The Trail of the Lonesome Pine." In the novel, one of the main characters is based on John Wright, who was close friends with the book's author. The character was named "Devil Judd Tolliver." The assertion that Devil John is based on Devil Judd, and not the other way around, is a ridiculous one.

Anyone familiar with the novel's characters and the very real people they're based on would recognize this immediately. For instance, *"Bad"* Rufe Tolliver, in the novel, is easily identified as **"Bad"** Talt Hall. Likewise, *"Old"* Buck Falin is based on **"Old"** Clabe Jones; *"Uncle"* Billy is based on **"Uncle"** Willie Wright, and so on. Obviously the nickname "Devil," given to the character based on John, is derived from the name John Fox Jr. knew him as . . . "Devil" John Wright!

Not to belabor the point --- beyond this there exists recorded stories where John is referred to as Devil John by the principles. Not only did these stories originate decades before the book was published, but some of these tales reveal that his reputation preceded him into other states, namely Virginia and West Virginia. The bottom line is that John Wright became Devil John Wright in the late 1870's, and was known as Devil John far and wide years before John Fox's novel ever existed!

Already a prolific writer, Fox had initially come to Appalachia to cash in through land dealings during the "coal boom" that began in the mid 1880's. Such endeavors would quickly lead him to Devil John Wright who, along with his official duties, was acting as a type of liaison between the coal companies and the region's landowners. By the "Trail of the Lonesome Pine's" publication in 1908, John had made a permanent home in Pound, Virginia and was working as a Deputy Sheriff and Jailer of Wise County. He was sixty-four years old when the book that brought him to national prominence was released. He, reportedly, never read the novel.

Aside from Devil John's career as a Deputy Sheriff it has long been held by some that he also became a U.S. Marshall. This does not seem to be the case. John's oldest and dearest friend, "Bad" Talt Hall, "The Terror of the Cumberlands," had, as incredible as it may seem, reportedly once been a U.S. Marshall As previously stated, the lives of John and Talt were so inextricably linked that their actions were constantly being confused one with the other. Adding to this may be the fact that Devil John's son, W. T. "Chid" Wright, always referred to his father as having been a "Federal Agent." What did he mean by this?

In 1850 a man named Allan Pinkerton started the famous (and infamous) Pinkerton Detective Agency. The company's logo was the "All Seeing Eye," combined with the motto "We Never Sleep." After thwarting an assassination attempt against President Abraham Lincoln, the agency was employed by the federal government to fulfill the duties performed in modern times by the U.S. Secret Service, regarding Executive protection.

With its mandate to operate under the auspices of the federal government, the Pinkerton Detective Agency grew rapidly to an entity that could enforce the law in many of the same respects as the U.S. Marshals. Indeed, the agency's ranks would eventually swell to a number of "Detectives" rivaled only by the standing Army of the United States In 1885, at the age of forty-one, Devil John Wright became a "Pinkerton Man." It is thought that this is the reason "Chid" Wright referred to his Dad as a "Federal Agent."

Devil John's reputation preceding him, Pinkerton was happy to have him join their ranks. For ten years John employed the attributes of a relentless man-hunter, accomplished woodsman and unequaled gunslinger in bringing to justice, dead or alive, the outlaws unfortunate enough to be assigned to him. He always got his man! As a result, Devil John was, more and more, given the "worst of the worst" to pursue. Along with this, the percentage of the reward money accorded to him for his work seemed to grow less and less. Lamenting these two reasons, Devil John eventually handed in his resignation to the main office located in Richmond, Virginia.

Coincidentally (or not) John would join the newly formed Baldwin Detective Agency whose main office was in Charleston, West Virginia, but had a satellite office located in Bluefield, West Virginia, closer to John's home. It was 1895.

William Baldwin had started the agency in the early 1890's. In 1900 he was joined by Thomas Felts. In 1910 the name of the enterprise was changed to the Baldwin-Felts Detective agency. In March of 1912 this agency was employed by the Governor of Virginia to apprehend members of the infamous "Allen family."

The Allens had shot-up the Carroll County Courthouse in Hillsville, Virginia. Five people were killed in this massacre, including the county's Prosecutor and Sheriff. Seven people were wounded. Having no Sheriff to chase down the murderers, the Governor called in Baldwin-Felts. The story dominated national news up to the sinking of the Titanic that same year. The unrelenting detectives eventually tracked down and arrested the Allen family members responsible for the crime, and they were brought to justice.

Though hailed as heroic for their endeavors in capturing the Allens, eight years later the Baldwin Felts Detective Agency would wax to infamy. To this day the name Baldwin-Felts is accursed by union workers in America, but most especially by coal miners.

On May 19th, 1920 thirteen Baldwin-Felts Detectives were in the coal town of Matewan in Mingo County, West Virginia. They'd been hired by the coal company to evict miners who'd been threatening unionization from the Big Stone coal camp. Matewan Chief of Police, Sid Hatfield along with Mayor Cabell Testerman, intercepted the detectives as they attempted to leave the town. The town's officers, flanked by several Matewan residents, wanted to stop the evictions. The Baldwin-Felts men were having none of it. Tempers flared, warrants were exchanged, and suddenly guns were fired! No one knows who shot first. When it was all over seven Baldwin-Felts Detectives lay dead, and four townspeople, including the mayor were killed. This event is known as the Matewan Massacre. Though the Police Chief escaped death that fateful day, a group of detectives would eventually kill him as he entered the courthouse in nearby Welch, West Virginia. The detectives were acquitted on a questionable claim of self-defense. This massacre, and subsequent atrocities on the part of coal companies, would galvanize the movement that led to the United Mine Workers of America and federal laws to protect the workers from the predatory practices of coal companies and others.

Devil John's participation in the two aforementioned exploits is not known, but highly doubtful. When the Allen Massacre in Carroll County happened John would've been sixty-eight years old. When the Matewan Massacre occurred he would've been a full seventy-six years old. It is likely that John resigned from the Baldwin Detective Agency around 1905. This is when Devil John made Wise County, Virginia his permanent residence, and became a Wise County Deputy and Jailer. It is thought that, by 1910, John had retired from being a lawman altogether.

The press of the early 20th century credited Devil John with varying numbers of men he killed. One article in the Mountain Eagle News, in Letcher County, claimed that he had twenty-eight notches on his gun and lamented that he'd not broke even by only killing twenty-eight, while fathering thirty-one (he actually fathered thirty-three). Some actually claimed he'd killed ninety-nine men, but this was the exact number, though obviously embellished, attributed to John's friend, "Bad" Talt Hall. Devil John himself claimed seven killings "outside of war." These were, presumably, legal killings. It is doubtful that John would've revealed any legally questionable killings. In the end, whatever the actual, terrible score was, it was a number Devil John took with him to his grave!

Talt

Thomas Talton (Talt) Hall was born in 1846, being two years younger than Devil John. He was a man of slight build, with black hair, who usually sported a mustache. He was forty-six years old at his death. Talt's family had been involved in more than their share of mountain feuds with other families in the area. Among these were the Maggards. When Talt was fourteen years old, just two years prior to entering the Civil War, his father, Dave Hall, arranged for his boy to be "blooded."

Dave Hall, along with a few others of his kin, had captured a feudal enemy named Henry Maggard. The Hall clan forced the hapless man to his knees next to a fallen tree. Dave gave his son a pistol, and forced the teenager to assassinate the middle-aged Maggard by shooting him in the back. Upon murdering the poor man, Talt reportedly leaped upon a split-rail fence, flapped his arms wildly, made a crowing noise then exclaimed, "From here on out, I'll be known as "Bad" Talt Hall!" And so he was!

By the end of his criminal career, when his neck was stretched at the first hanging to occur in Wise County, Virginia, September 2, 1892, "Bad" Talt Hall was claimed to be responsible for ninety-nine deaths. This number is generally believed to be a gross embellishment, however, it gained Talt Hall the moniker of "Bad" Talt Hall, "The Terror of the Cumberlands!"

After the war, it is reported that Bad Talt was actually a Deputy Sherriff of Floyd County, Kentucky for two years. He also pulled a stint as a U.S. Marshall for the Eastern District of Kentucky. How many men he just flat-out murdered as a matter of course, along with those legally brought in, dead or alive, as a bona fide lawman may have been a noteworthy score, but not likely to have been ninety-nine. Like Devil John, when asked about his killings outside of war, both men low-balled the estimate to less than ten apiece. The actual number of men gunned down by Devil John and Bad Talt probably falls anywhere in a terrible span between ten and a hundred. There simply are no records with which to come to a more exact tally.

As to Bad Talt Hall, the record that does exist reveals that he was sought or arrested for, and subsequently exonerated of, the murders of four men. Along with these can be added a fifth whom Hall, though never arrested for, had unquestionably committed. It is universally believed that Bad Talt Hall, absolutely, was guilty of all five of the murders he was accused of perpetrating. He escaped justice, time and time again, through the intimidation he, and others (most likely including Devil John) brought to bear against witnesses, juries and law enforcement.

Prior to his execution, Bad Talt did finally confess to committing four of the five murders for which he'd been accused. The fifth victim, Frank Sayler (some places record his last name as Salyer), murdered March 6th, 1885, Hall refused to confess to killing. This is notable in that Bad Talt was not only, unquestionably guilty in the murder, but it was this crime that would ultimately lead to Hall's sixth, and final, murder. His sixth, and last, recorded victim, Police Chief E. B. Hylton, would be the one murder for which he, finally, paid the ultimate price. Aside from this, it would actually be the previous, fifth murder of Frank Sayler, that would provide one of the sparks for the infamous Wright-Jones feud of the 1880's.

The question may be asked. What was the impetus for Bad Talt Hall killing Frank Sayler, thus setting in motion events leading to a bloody mountain feud, the murder of a peace officer and his own demise by the hang-man's noose? As strange as it may seem, simply stated, it was love. At some point Bad Talt Hall came to be enamored with Frank Sayler's wife (her name is lost to history). Not long after beginning an affair with this woman, Frank Sayler was conveniently found murdered, and Bad Talt immediately took her, and her children, to live with him. The couple, though not married, lived as man and wife.

This event did not sit well with two notable individuals. These would be Talt's sworn enemy, and infamous Sheriff of Knott County, Kentucky, "Ol' Clabe" Claibourne Jones, and Frank Sayler's brother-in-law, the Chief of Police of Norton, Virginia, and Talt's final victim, E. B. Hylton. Hylton reportedly vowed vengeance for his wife's brother's killing, and Ol' Clabe Jones set-out to arrest Bad Talt for Sayler's murder. With the murder of Bad Talt's rival for the "Sayler woman's" (as she is called) affections, the die was cast for the murder, mayhem and mountain justice that ensued. Caught squarely in the middle of these events was Bad Talt Hall's best friend and closest comrade, Devil John Wright!

The particulars of the friendship, the "where, how and whys," between Devil John and Bad Talt are purposefully vague. In short, these two men conducted much of their relationship clandestinely. The reasons for this make perfect sense. First, and foremost, mountaineers of that time kept their "business" to themselves. Secondly, the relationship of Devil John and Bad Talt was the discrepant friendship of an outlaw, Bad Talt, with a lawman, Devil John. It was a friendship that caused Devil John to look the other way regarding Bad Talt's perpetual status as a wanted criminal. Indeed, Devil John was depended upon to provide financial aid, protective cover and use of violence in the defense of his friend, time and time again. This even included creating a fake grave which Devil John claimed held Bad Talt's remains, when, in fact, Devil John had given his friend money and instructions to leave the region. Unfortunately, this, and other ruses, were always thwarted by Bad Talt's refusal to simply stay away. Like a bad penny, Bad Talt would always turn up. In this regard, Bad Talt Hall was his own worst enemy. The obvious question of why did Devil John align himself so closely with, and took so many chances for his friend is a valid one with only one (somewhat unsatisfying) answer . . . the war!

It may be recalled that John Wesley Wright and Thomas Talton Hall were inducted on the same day, at the same place and into the same unit of the Confederate Army, the Thirteenth (then called the Tenth) Kentucky Cavalry. Bad Talt was only sixteen at the time. It is possible that Devil John, being two years older, felt a big brother type of affection for the younger man from his own "neck of the woods."

Aside from the recorded induction, and the Wright family's contention that this is where their friendship began, there are no preserved records, traditions or stories of the duo's war experience together. Indeed, in the account of the Thirteenth Kentucky Cavalry's defeat and subsequent capture at the Battle of Gladesville, during which Devil John made his memorable escape, in July of 1863, any mention of Private Thomas Talton Hall is conspicuously missing.

In light of this it may be wondered. Did Devil John and Bad Talt have a pre-existing friendship prior to the war? After all, they did grow up in the same area. It would be a doubtful contention that the two didn't, at the very least, know of each other before their enrollment into the Confederate Army on October 4th, 1862. Were Devil John and Bad Talt childhood friends? It's left an open, and probably unanswerable question. There is no tradition or record to either prove, or disprove such a contention. What is known is that the sixteen year old young man encountered by a young Devil John at enlistment, in the person of Bad Talt Hall, already had the blood of, at least, one cold-blooded murder on his young hands. This was the aforementioned assassination of Henry Maggard committed, two years prior to enlistment, by a fourteen year old Talt Hall, at his own father's behest.

While the notion of the American outlaw has been somewhat romanticized in popular literature, and the likes of Bad Talt Hall is no exception, the truth is more often than not an unsavory one. Bad Talt Hall had four hallmarks which defined his career as an outlaw, and would lead to his inevitable end. These were a propensity for violence, a complete disregard for law enforcement, a weakness for illicit sexual relationships and, perhaps most notably, alcoholism Indeed, he went to his reward completely intoxicated to the point that there was an actual fear that his tremendous alcohol consumption, while awaiting execution, was such that it would allow him to beat the gallows in his death

As to his propensities for violence and total disregard for law enforcement is concerned, it would be the gunning down of a Police Chief that resulted in Bad Talt's execution. Though given a large sum of money by Devil John, and agreeing to abscond to Canada to start a new life; Bad Talt defied his friend's admonishment to stay away from the "Sayler woman," and immediately joined her in Memphis, Tennessee. It was in Memphis, blowing his cover upon sending one of the Sayler children to a local saloon for booze, that Bad Talt Hall was captured Had he taken Devil John's advice, along with the money, it is likely that Bad Talt Hall could've lived out his days in safe, alcoholic anonymity in another country. Instead, it was his weakness for the "Sayler woman" that, not only, created the "bad blood" between Bad Talt and the police officer whom he murdered, but his subsequent capture, trial and execution as well. As stated, it was the unlikely reason of his love for a woman that would be the ruination of Bad Talt Hall.

Prior to the killing of the Norton police Chief, "Ol Clabe" Jones, from Knott County, along with his men (kin), pursued Bad Talt for Frank Sayler's murder. Rather than flee, Bad Talt gathered his own men (kin), and fought back. The result was years of attack, capture, escape and counter attack played-out in Letcher county and the Eastern, Kentucky region. It was inevitable that Devil John would enter the fray. In short order, though the disputes originated with Bad Talt, Devil John assumed a principle role against Ol' Clabe and his men. The result was what is known as the Wright-Jones feud of the 1880's. These events will be explored in more depth in "The Feuds" chapter.

It is the murder of Police Chief E. B. Hylton, and the resulting trial and execution, which gained Bad Talt Hall his infamous place in Appalachian history. Just as in modern times, the popular press seized upon the historic trial and execution of Bad Talt Hall. Reporters came from as far away as Lynchburg, Virginia to cover the story. The more "civilized" populace east of the mountains was curious about the successful application of American jurist prudence in the "wild and wooly" Appalachian mountains of the 1890's. It must be remembered that this was the era of the "feuding hillbilly" popularized in the popular mind-set by turn of the century media coverage of such events as the ongoing Hatfield-McCoy feud.

The town of Gladeville had recently undergone the name change to Wise, Virginia and been installed as the seat of the county bearing the same name. The trial of Bad Talt would be the first test of the region's ability to administer justice in the manner which was a standard to the rest of the country. In short, the question was one of whether American, or mountain justice would prevail!

Along with this, there was the open question and real concern that Bad Talt would either be rescued, or preemptively shot before being hanged, thus thwarting justice. The person most feared, by the masses, of accomplishing this was none other than Devil John Wright. It would be the particulars of all of these lawful circumstances that the famous American author, John Fox Jr., would employ in the climax of his acclaimed novel "The Trail of the Lonesome Pine." Thus, the criminal career, arrest, trial and execution of Bad Talt Hall would be further immortalized in the region's and nation's psyche

In conclusion, consider the following excerpt from The Lynchburg News, dated September 1st, 1892. Unfortunately, the name of the reporter was not given.

"Talton Hall's criminal record has probably never been paralleled in the United States. He is credited with 99 murders, and while this is an exaggeration, there is no doubt that he is responsible for the deaths of 8 or 10 men. He was born in Letcher County, Kentucky, 46 years ago, and grew up with such desperadoes as John Wright, who is credited with 27 murders, and Doc Taylor, against whom he is now so bitter. These men joined General Morgan's band when the war broke out, and made themselves conspicuous for their deeds of reckless daring."

"The jail is under heavy guard and picket lines have been thrown out on all the roads leading to the town. If any of Hall's friends attempt to interfere there may be some bloodshed, but nothing short of a general uprising can stop, or delay the execution of sentence."

FEUDS

It's an unfortunate fact of history that the region of Eastern Kentucky, where Devil John was born and raised, is well known for the "feuds" which raged within the area from pre-war, up to modern times. Much has been offered as explanation of why this particular region was rife with belligerent, long-lasting and violent "wars" erupting between individuals, only to spill-over into whole populations in the region. Indeed, citizens bearing no kinship to the parties involved in a "feud" would have to choose sides at times just to "get along" in their communities. Nowhere is this better exemplified than the infamous Hatfield-McCoy feud which involved so many people feuding across the state line between Kentucky and West Virginia, that it almost sparked an actual war between the two states!

It's also an unfortunate fact that, to this day, sorting out the precise history regarding any of the Appalachian feuds which occurred in the 19th century is a daunting task at best. The very nature of these conflicts, with varying details dependent upon the relationship to the feuding parties of whomever relates the events, possesses an inherent bias which is reflected in the different histories given for the same circumstances. In other words, the given history of a feud is dependent much of the time upon which "side" of the conflict those relating the facts choose to align with. Then, along with any bias, the secretive nature of the mountain folk themselves, being reticent to acknowledge the particular facts of a feud, simply "muddies the waters" further regarding any historical facts. In this, Devil John's participation in "feuding" is no exception. There seems to be as many different versions of the feuds he was involved in, as there are varied sources relating the history of those feuds. Bearing all of this in mind, the topic is approached here.

It seems that Devil John became a principle actor in, at least, two separate feuds. In both cases it can be surmised that he believed he was acting in the authorized capacity of an agent or officer of the law, and to a certain extent this was actually true. For example, in the famous "Wright - Jones" conflict, Devil John held a $500 warrant for his nemesis, Clabe (Claib) Jones' arrest that was signed by the Governor of Kentucky. However, Clabe Jones also held an identical warrant for Devil John, signed by the same Governor. Such was the confusing state of affairs which became the status quo for many of the Eastern Kentucky feuds. It is also notable that all of the feuds, including the ones Devil John was involved with, usually began as vendettas of vengeance between individuals, including neighbors and relatives, which spread to friends and acquaintances of the feuding parties who, voluntarily or not, had to take sides. It was this attribute of the feud that, more or less, forced Devil John to become involved, quickly escalating him to be a chief participant, and final arbiter in both of the conflicts in which he participated. These two "feuds" he became involved with are known under different titles, but the most popular would be the "Wright - Jones Feud" of the 1880's, and the "K.K.K. War" which occurred at the turn of the 20th century.

The Jones - Wright Feud

As with most of the mountain feuds, the beginnings of the Jones-Wright feud are a bit convoluted, but can be, initially, ascribed to the dealings of one man, namely, Devil John's lifelong comrade Talton (Bad Talt) Hall. Evidently, Talt Hall had members of his "gang" attempt to kill a man with whom Hall held a grudge, by throwing him from the third story window of a hotel as he slept. A man was, indeed, thrown to his death that fateful night, but the killers had picked the wrong victim in the darkness of the hotel room. The intended victim, Richard Vance, quickly avenged the attempt on his life (and errant murder of his hapless traveling companion) when the brother of Talt Hall, Andrew, was killed by him a short time later. One of Vance's friends, who was supposedly involved in the killing of Andrew Hall, was a man named Linville Higgins. In equally short order, Linville Higgins was murdered out of revenge for the death of Talt Hall's brother!

The revenge killing of Linville Higgins took place near Hindman, Kentucky, under the jurisdiction of an infamous lawman named Claibourne (Ol' Clabe) Jones. Three men had been positively identified in the murder of Linville Higgins, including Samuel ('Kinky-haired Sam') Wright. This was the younger brother of Devil John Wright. At some later point in all of this web of vengeance and murder, Talt Hall himself would be wanted for the untimely death of a man named Frank Sayler whose widow had become Hall's lover. Reportedly, Ol' Clabe Jones eventually held a warrant for Talt's arrest as well as the alleged murderers of Linville Higgins, all of whom lived under the protection of lawman Devil John Wright in Letcher County. Devil John, by virtue of his relationship to the men wanted by Clabe Jones, was firmly drawn into the fray. As stated, it wasn't long before Ol' Clabe and Devil John both had warrants, signed by the Governor, for each other. Thus began a running conflict that would last for years between factions of lawmen, mountaineers and "posses" in the two Eastern Kentucky counties led by the Knott County lawman Clabe Jones against Letcher county lawman Devil John Wright.

On a few occasions Clabe Jones and his "gang" would steal into Letcher County, surround a cabin and open fire as the inhabitants emerged to do their daily chores. This tactic met with little success as far as capturing any of the fugitives Clabe had warrants for, and was generally a waste of time and ammunition. The cabins (called "forts") were built with thick logs and woodwork which was, basically, impervious to gunfire.

Conversely, Devil John and his "gang" would travel under stealth to Clabe's home-place, meeting the same circumstance and stalemate. It was even reported that, on one particular night, the two groups actually passed by each other unknowingly en route to attack their respective "forts." As a result, the feud was relegated to sparse, but violent encounters between individuals at various locations throughout the region which, reportedly, would come to involve over a hundred and fifty people. As the feud dragged on, the citizenry became weary of the violence, and demanded a resolution to the conflict.

Just as the seminal events for the feud began in a hotel room, the resolution would follow suit. Devil John and Ol' Clabe agreed to disarm and lodge together, in the same room at a Jenkins, Kentucky hotel in Letcher County, until they worked out terms to end the hostilities. The pair dropped their charges against each other, and Devil John guaranteed the men wanted for the Higgins murder, including his own brother, "Kinky Haired" Sam, would stand trial. Clabe agreed to these terms, and gave his word he would abide by the court's decision in the case.

Both men did, indeed, keep their word in this regard. A trial was held, and the men accused of the murder, including Devil John's brother, were quickly acquitted upon corroborating testimonies that none of the accused were in the region at the time of the murder. Though this was not the verdict Clabe and his men had desired, Ol' Clabe Jones kept his word, and took no further action in the matter. Thus, the Wright - Jones Feud was ended, but not before being so ingrained in local history that twenty years later the author (and good friend of Devil John Wright), John Fox Jr., would immortalize the affair as the fictional "Falin - Tolliver Feud" in his best-selling novel, "The Trail of the Lonesome Pine!"

The K.K.K. War

A little more than a decade after the Wright - Jones Feud was settled, a new and terrible circumstance arose in Letcher County. A group (some would say "gang") of young men, some of which being from the best known of families, formed a "klavern" of the Ku Klux Klan in the region. In no time at all, this group would begin "night-rides" whilst costumed in ghoulish and ghost-like disguises. The aim of the night-rides was to exert "vigilante justice" upon citizens the group considered to be immoral, or of ill repute, and exert "correction" upon the chosen victims. What actually occurred was a reign of sadistic beating, whipping and robbing of folks, women in particular, under cover of night throughout the county!

Devil John managed to avoid the growing conflict between the KKK and those in Letcher County who were opposed to it, including members of the Sheriff's department whom were John's own kinsmen. One reason for his reticence to get involved was the unsavory fact that other relatives of John's, including a nephew, were actually Klansmen themselves Having blood relatives on each side of the growing conflict made it incredibly hard for Devil John to measure his response to the whole matter. That is, until the activities of the KKK resulted in the cold-blooded murder of John's cousin, Deputy Sheriff William S. Wright and a woman whom John, undoubtedly, had been romantically involved with, as well as the woman's son. Her name was Jemima Hall who, reportedly, had run a "brothel" in Letcher County. The KKK killed her and her teenaged son in a gun battle which broke-out when the Klan had gone to her home to issue their form of justice one cold autumn night in 1900 For Devil John, it was the "tipping point," and he set himself to bring an end to the KKK's reign of terror!

It should be unsurprising that the struggle with the KKK is a touchy subject to this day. Indeed, there are good people who currently reside in Letcher County, Kentucky who never knew that one or more of their ancestors was ever involved with the Klan. This ignorance of the particulars of the whole affair might be due to the fact that many of the participants were quite young, and would consider their participation to not be a reason for boasting later in life. Additionally, some of the Klansmen who would face justice for their role, including murder, would later be pardoned for their crimes. One of these men, Noah Reynolds, who, along with his brothers, John and Morgan, had been convicted for their crimes, would actually write a highly skewed, false account of the KKK War, choosing to label the struggle, instead, as the "Wright-Reynolds Feud." In Noah Reynolds dubious account the victims of the Klan violence, including Deputy Sheriff William S. Wright and his son Willie, were blamed for their own demise. Noah Reynolds also managed to write this defected historical revision of the events without one mention of the KKK of which he, and his brothers, were actually leaders!

Devil John's response to the KKK would be to gather certain members of his family, including his sons, and trusted friends in a "posse" that spent months tracking down and arresting individual Klan members. Aside from this, there are varied reports of two all-out gunfights occurring between the KKK and John's group. This includes a final battle fought near the modern area known as Yont's Fork in Letcher County. It would be in this final engagement that Devil John's young relative and son of the murdered policeman, William S. Wright, Willie Wright, would be mortally wounded One of the leading Klansmen, John Reynolds, would be gravely wounded by Devil John, and lose the use of his right arm for life. The rest of the Klansmen, including the aforementioned Noah Reynolds, and John's own nephew, Creed Potter, would be routed and subsequently arrested on later dates. In spite of charges brought against the accused Klansmen, and some trials being conducted, virtually all of the accused managed to either avoid their due sentences, or never be tried at all   The entire matter was summarily forgotten (some might say "covered up") within a few years of the coal industry "booming" in the area.

The
Prodigious
Progenitor

Devil John Wright became legendary for many of his attributes and pursuits, but none are more remarkable than his personal relations (for lack of a better word) with the opposite sex. In his lifetime he maintained a "polygamous" lifestyle with, no less than, seven women! This included two sets of sisters. As a result of these "marriages" (for lack of a better word) he would father thirty-three children! The firstborn of these being James, born when John was a twenty-one year old Confederate soldier, then up to Kedrick, who was fathered fifty years later when John was seventy-one! Beyond the seven women, whom were referred to by John and others as his "wives," were an untold number of affairs with many, many other women, throughout his eighty-seven year lifetime!

Obviously, there's much which can be said regarding Devil John's views concerning fidelity. However, realizing that my own existence, as his great, great grandson, is due to his "propensities" toward the women in his life, any indictment of his moral standards in this regard might seem disingenuous at best. The questions regarding the 'moralities" his "love-life" (many though they may be) are properly left for others to explore and opine upon. The facts, the relationships and resulting children, are what they are, and offered here as simple historicity of those conceptions absent any editorial.

The first of these women, who was also the first "legal" wife of John's until her death, was Martha "Mattie" Humphrey. John and Mattie met as a result of John being wounded in the Battle of Cynthiana in 1864. In 1865 Mattie gave birth to John's first child, James, and the couple was married in Cynthiana, Kentucky on October 14th, 1866. In 1875 Mattie gave birth to her and John's second (and last) child together, Johnny Philip, while residing in Letcher County, Kentucky. The historical record suggests that around this time Mattie became somewhat incapacitated, mentally speaking, and would remain so until her death in 1924 at the age of eighty-six. The cause of her death is listed simply as "senility," but John had made statements regarding her lack of capacity throughout their marriage. Sadly, their youngest son, Johnny Philip, would be murdered in 1875 at the age of twenty-three, and their oldest, James, would die in 1914 of natural causes at the age of fifty. Both parents outlived their children.

The next two women ("wives") Devil John was involved with were actually sisters. This would be Surrilda and Margaret Austin of Letcher County. Surrilda was, like Mattie, seven years older than John, and bore him a daughter, named Margaret (named after her sister) in 1866. Surrilda's younger sister, Margaret, would also give birth to a daughter by Devil John, named Mahala, that very same year John and Margaret were both twenty-two at the time. The older sister, Surrilda, would bear two more children, both sons, to John. These would be Enoch, born in 1870, and Martin, born that next year. The following year, 1872, the younger Austin sister, Margaret, would bear a final son to Devil John named Mack.

The fourth of Devil John's "wives" was Mary Bentley, thirteen years younger than John, she bore her first of eight children by him when she was nineteen, and John was thirty-two. This would be the first of John's seven daughters by Mary Bentley, her name was Flora. She was born in 1876. The next daughter by Mary Bentley was Liza, born in 1878. Then, in 1881 Alice was born. Three years later, in 1884, Mary Bentley gave birth to Easter. Two years after this, in 1886, Elizabeth would be born. Another two years, in 1888, the only son Mary Bentley bore to

John came into the world. His name was Samuel. Four years after Samuel's birth, in 1892, Myrtle was born. Seven years later, in 1899, Mary Bentley bore her last child to Devil John, a girl named Mallie. The following year, 1900, Mary Bentley died of cancer. She was forty-three years old.

The next of Devil John's "wives" was, if the number of children born is an indicator, his favorite. This would be Alice Lee Harmon who gave John eleven children, eight sons and three daughters, the oldest of which is my great grandmother Alice Harmon was born in 1878. When she was sixteen years old she bore her first child to the, then, fifty year old Devil John. This would be the oldest of her sons, Frank, born August 1, 1894. Next would be Bertha, my great, grandmother, born in 1896. A year later William T. "Chid" Wright was born. A third son, Conrad was born two years later, in 1899. Another daughter, Elizabeth (who died in infancy) was born in 1901.

In the year 1903 she gave birth to another son, Clarence, but lost four year old Conrad to disease. In 1905 another son, Chester was born, but he also died in infancy. In 1907 she gave birth to a sixth son, named Carlous. Two years after this she gave birth to a third daughter, Maudie. In 1913 she gave birth to another son, Charles Roe. Then, in 1915, she bore the last of her eleven children by Devil John, a final son named Kedrick. Alice was thirty-eight when Kedrick Wright was born, Devil John was seventy-one and had, at that ripe old age, fathered his final child Moreover, just as was the case with the Austin sisters, John would father children by Alice Harmon's older sister, "Ol'" India Harmon The record concerning India Harmon, and her children is unfortunately lacking of verifiable details. What does seem to be the case is that this older sister of Alice Harmon bore Devil John four daughters. This would be Virgie, born in 1895 and died around 1909, Rose, born in 1898, Alma, born in 1904 and a fourth daughter, Jenny, for which all records are, conspicuously, missing. Alice Lee Harmon died in 1926, at the age of forty-six.

After being turned down for marriage in the summer of 1924 by Alice Harmon, John would legally marry his last wife, Ellen Sanders (also listed as "Saunders"), on September 4th, 1924, less than six months after Mattie's death. John was eighty years of age, and his bride was sixty-one, being born in 1863. Though legally married in 1924, Ellen Sanders had already born four children to John, three boys and one girl, who were already middle-aged at the time of the marriage These were Joel, born in 1883, Daniel, born in 1885, a girl named Healthy, born in 1887 and finally, Ira born in 1889 If a count has been kept, by the 1924 marriage of John Wesley Wright to Ellen Sanders, Devil John had fathered, at least, thirty-three children (thirty-four if the daughter, Jenny, by India Harmon's included) by seven women beginning at the age of twenty, with his firstborn son, James, by Mattie, up to his last-born son, Kedrick, by Alice Harmon . . . fifty-one years later.

Reportedly, Ellen Sanders had converted to Christianity, and was a member of the "Old" Regular Baptist Church. Within five years of marrying Devil John, she had caused him to, also, be converted. On July 24th, 1929, witnessed by a crowd in excess of two-thousand people, John Wesley Wright was baptized in Bald Camp Creek, at Fairview, Virginia. He would have no use, nor allow the use in his presence, of his famous nickname, "Devil," ever again!

About one and a half years later, on January 30th, 1931 John Wesley Wright passed away quietly at his home at Horse Gap in Pound, Virginia. He was three months shy of his eighty-seventh birthday. Seventeen years later, in 1948, his wife, Ellen, would join him in death, and is buried beside him at the family cemetery at the old home-place at Horse Gap.

The 'Tale' of the Lonesome Pine

The novel "The Trail of the Lonesome Pine" was first published in 1908. It has the distinction of being one of the first million copy bestsellers in American history. Not only did this propel the book's author, John Fox Jr., into the national spotlight, but the man upon whom one of the novel's main characters was based as well. This was Devil John Wright, who is depicted as the "giant" mountaineer "Devil Judd Tolliver."

The book would spawn three motion pictures. One of these was an early effort at direction by an acclaimed movie director, the iconic Cecil B. Demille. Another, filmed in 1936, being the first outdoor Technicolor film ever made, would include the film debut of a young actor named Henry Fonda. Unfortunately, this film adaptation, directed by Henry Hathaway, bore little resemblance to Fox's novel. Along with these would be a 1912 Broadway production, and no less than two hit songs, all based on the book.

"The Trail of the Lonesome Pine," spans a time frame of, approximately, ten years between 1884 and 1894. However, it derives from events, central to its theme, which occurred up to 1908 when it was originally published. The prime example of this would be the dealings between the coal companies (most notably the Consolidated Coal and Coke Co.) and the landowners of the region. From 1900 to 1916 Devil John acted as a liaison/negotiator between the local citizenry, who'd come to trust and respect him, and the coal companies, which compensated him handsomely, in the brokering of land and mineral rights during the "Coal Boom" at the turn of the 20th century.

In 1904 Devil John, himself, sold vast amounts of his own holdings in Kentucky, and settled permanently at Horse Gap, on the outskirts of Pound in Wise County, Virginia. It was this event that is the basis for one of the major themes in John Fox Jr.'s novel. This would be the mountaineer character based on Devil John, named "Devil" Judd Tolliver, making his fortune off of the coal found in his land.

It would be the lure of such fortune that originally led the author of "The Trail of the Lonesome Pine," John Fox Jr., to settle in Wise county, Virginia in 1885. Such interests would inevitably lead him to local "movers and shakers" like Devil John who, at the time, resided just across the state line on Elkhorn Creek in Letcher county, Kentucky.

Indeed, Fox's keen knowledge in such dealings is superbly reflected in the protagonist of the novel, Jack Hale. Hale dreamed of prosperity for himself, and the town he helped to create through such dealings of industrialization and modernization in the region. The novel portrays it as a dream that would become, in many ways, tantamount to the serpent being unleashed in the Garden of Eden. The novel presents a historically accurate theme of a "boom-town gone bust." This is a theme actually reflected by Fox's hometown of Big Stone Gap, from which Fox derived most of the attributes of the novel's fictional town known simply as "The Gap."

While the shared interests of land brokering and bringing "civilization" to the "hills" was the impetus for John Fox Jr. And Devil John's relationship, it would bloom into a close, enduring friendship. It would be Devil John's tales and way of life that is an obvious inspiration for much of the novel's narrative. Likewise, Fox would come to an intimate knowledge of Devil John's contemporaries and family members, whom he used as a basis for the characters populating his famous novel.

John Fox Jr. was an author during the American "naturalism movement" in writing popularized after the Civil War into the first half of the 20th century. Fox employed the "local color" genre in his writing, also popular at the time. This method is where authors would employ the use of actual persons, places and events in a "mix" as the basis for their fictional characters, landscapes and themes in their writing. This is precisely what "The Trail of the Lonesome Pine" represents. The book employs a blending of multiple, "real" people to flesh out a single character, or a mix of locations to derive a single place and a set of actual events, blended with fancy, to drive the story.

This has led to some confusion when trying to nail down the exact identities of persons, places and things Fox relied upon in his writing. Indeed, the silent, main character of the novel, the "Lonesome Pine's" actual existence has been a source of regional dispute for over a hundred years. Fortunately, this mystery, along with much of where Fox actually gained his inspiration for most of the book's characters, locations and themes can be unraveled by an in depth knowledge of the personal history and times of Devil John Wright.

A good example of this would be "The Trail of the Lonesome Pine's" characters of Squire Billy Beams and his wife, Ol' Hon. This couple is presented as the only neighbors of the book's heroine, June Tolliver, who lives with her father, Devil Judd Tolliver, her stepmother and little brother in her father's cabin. Devil Judd's home is described as being located down the mountain topped by the "Lonesome Pine," and situated in "Lonesome Cove" by "Lonesome Creek." Just downstream, Squire Billy and Ol' Hon run a grist mill off of the creek. June calls Squire Billy, "Uncle" Billy. The meaning is clear. He is either the brother of her biological mother, who has no mention in the book, or he is the older brother of her Dad, Devil Judd. The latter is the best contention.

When Fox first encountered Devil John Wright, he resided in a cabin on Elkhorn Creek with his wife Mattie and any number of Devil John's children, including those to whom Mattie would be considered a "stepmother." Devil John's closest neighbors on Elkhorn Creek were his brother, "Kinky Haired" Sam Wright and his wife, Martha. Here, the couple ran . . . a grist mill!

The most obvious discrepancy between the fictional Uncle Billy and Ol' Hon, and the real life "Kinky Haired" Sam and his wife Martha, is that the couple in the novel are portrayed as a kindly, elderly couple. "Kinky Haired" Sam and Martha were, in reality, much younger than Devil John. It is more likely than not that Fox blended an actual elderly couple known by him personally, but lost to history, with the people he, undoubtedly, encountered during his many visits to Devil John's home in Kentucky. It is a classic example of the "local color" genre being employed in its blending and mixing of characters and story components from real life counterparts.

As stated, it is this blending that has resulted in much speculation, and even dissension amongst folks claiming that their respective ancestor or relative just had to be the sole basis for some of the book's characters. Beyond this, matters of civic pride have entered the fray regarding which town is Fox's "The Gap" based upon? Was there ever a real "lonesome Pine?" If so, which mountain did the "Lonesome Pine" adorn? There is even a question as to which state, Virginia or Kentucky, did any of this really occur? Local figures, writers and historians have argued these questions for over a century.

For instance, "The Gap" is the town where much of the novel's action plays out. Because of obvious descriptions in the book, including named locations and structures, it has long been supposed that "The Gap" is actually Fox's hometown of Big Stone Gap, Virginia.

Indeed, this identification has resulted in Big Stone Gap putting on a perennial outdoor drama since 1964 of "The Trail of the Lonesome Pine" during the summer months. It's been adapted as a musical performed by the locals, and has been actually designated as the official state outdoor drama for Virginia.

However, a detailed look at Fox's "Gap" reveals details of geography, history and incidentals that clearly show "The Gap" is based, not just on one, but four, separate towns in the region. These are unquestionably the towns of Norton, Pound (then called Pound Gap), the county seat of Wise and, finally, Big Stone Gap itself All of these are located within a twenty mile radius in Wise county, Virginia.

Part and parcel with the book's fame are myriad business and civic concerns sporting titles like "Trail" and "Lonesome Pine" in their names. A prime example is the hospital where the movie star Elizabeth Taylor once received emergency treatment. This was after a choking incident, famously parodied by John Belushi on Saturday Night Live, which the famous actress suffered in Big Stone Gap while dining with her, then, husband, Virginia State Senator John Warner. Naturally, the hospital is called Lonesome Pine Hospital! Another example would be the Lonesome Pine Scenic By-Way. The local Boy Scouts are part of the Lonesome Pine District. The list goes on and on. "The Trail of the Lonesome Pine" has taken on a huge role in the society of America that exists within the region of southwest Virginia, Eastern Kentucky, as far north as Beckley, West Virginia and southward into the Smoky Mountains of Eastern Tennessee

Jack Hale

The protagonist of the novel is John, "Jack" to his friends, Hale. This main character seems to be a composite of no less than three individual men, including John Fox Jr. himself. Jack Hale is presented as an "engineer" who originated from his hometown of Lexington, Kentucky, where he attended Transylvania University. He has settled in the idyllic, pre-industrial mountain hamlet called "The Gap." He envisions growing rich and modernizing The Gap by brokering deals with the local mountaineers for harvesting the vast coal and iron deposits held within their lands. Unfortunately, by the novel's end, Hale's good intentions and lofty expectations begin to be consumed by the "coal boom" he, himself, ignites.

The comparison of Hale to his creator, Fox, is easily made in this regard. As previously stated, Fox came to the region twenty-three years prior to his novel's publication. He was following the exact ambition as his character. John Fox Jr. also attended Transylvania University, but would eventually graduate with a major in English from Harvard. He, like Hale, was a "furriner" (foreigner), as the mountain folk called those not native to their mountains. He, like Hale, fell in love with the region, being enchanted by its people and environs. Unlike Hale, John Fox Jr. Did not do that well at brokering land deals, but, just as his character, he experienced the romance of his life while living in the "hills." Indeed, "The Trail of the Lonesome Pine" is nothing if not a timeless romance!

While his character, Hale, finds love in the person of Devil Judd's free-spirited, pseudo-feral, but highly intelligent (and beautiful) daughter, June Tolliver; Fox fell in love with renown Austrian opera diva, Fritzi Scheff. Fox actually dedicated his famous novel to "F. S." (Fritzi Scheff), and the couple was married just after the book's 1908 publication. Their torrid romance would not, however, have a happy ending. By all reports Fritzi loathed living in the little mountain town to which Fox took her home. The couple divorced in 1913 after just five years of marriage. Six years later, on July 8th, 1919, John Fox Jr. died of complications due to pneumonia. He was interred in his hometown near Paris, Kentucky just south of Cincinnati, Ohio. It is generally thought that, even though the novel's heroine, June, is not solely based on Fritzi, certainly Fox's descriptions of the romance between Jack and June reflects the degree to which Fox had been smitten by the feisty, Austrian-born cosmopolite.

In his lifetime John Fox Jr. Produced eleven, notable literary works. His first novel, "The Kentuckians," was published in 1897. The following year he worked as a correspondent in the Spanish-American War. From 1904 to 1905 he worked as a correspondent in the Russo-Japanese War. While his books and stories eclipsed his career as a journalist, it is notable that he originally worked in 1883 as a reporter in New York City. Likewise, the Hale character is portrayed as having connections in, and making visits to the Northern metropolis. In the end, Fox died a rich man, having sold over two-million copies of "The Trail of the Lonesome Pine," alone, in the eleven years prior to his death.

Beyond the obvious blending of his own life in the Jack Hale character, there is a second source that must be considered. It has long been reported, and remains so on the "Trail of the Lonesome Pine" outdoor drama's official webpage, that a certain geologist (and contemporary of Fox) named James Hodge, brought a young girl out of a local back-country coal camp, and enrolled her into school in Big Stone Gap. Here he remained her "sponsor" and provided for her education. The uncanny resemblance to elements of Jack Hale and June Tolliver's relationship cannot be overlooked. While there is some question as to the veracity of the story, it's blending into Fox's narrative would be in keeping with the "local color" genre with which he wrote "The Trail of the Lonesome Pine." This and, if the story's true, the congruity of the two tales would make the odds of it being sheer coincidence astronomical!

The third source of the Hale character seems to be a young man who courted, and eventually married one of Devil John's daughters, named William Church. William, like the "Uncle Billy" character was known as "Squire Billy." He was a man who, in spite of his youth, was installed as an overseer in constructing train trestles, but, like Hale, referred to himself as an "engineer." Accordingly, his preference of dress closely resembles Fox's description of Hale's attire. Most tellingly, when William Church approached Devil John with his notion of marrying his daughter, effectively removing her from her duties at the house; Devil John's original reply is practically a word for word quote of the Devil Judd character's original response to Hale taking June away to The Gap for schooling.

The Tollivers

It has long been established that the Tolliver "clan" of the novel is based on Devil John's kin, the Wright family. Even the surname Tolliver, and its derivative, Tollifaero (also described in the novel), are common Christian names within the Wright family contemporaneous with Devil John. During the friendship between John Fox Jr. and Devil John Wright, that spanned twenty years, Fox paid many visits to both of Devil John's homes. It would be at these locations that Fox would come to be intimately knowledgeable of all of Devil John's family members who were spoken of, lived nearby, or actually lived with Devil John, as was common to the clannish people of the region.

These locations included the home on Elkhorn Creek in Kentucky, and the home at Horse Gap, near Pound, Virginia. It would be these two locations, in both states, that Fox would blend into the memorable, fictional cabin at Lonesome Cove, on Lonesome Creek . . . in the shadow of the Lonesome Pine!

The small road that used to lead from the small community, then known as Pound Gap, up to Devil John's home at the base of the mountain creating the eastern flank of Horse Gap, is now a roadway intersected by the modern four-lane highway of U.S. 23. This nondescript, little road, which Fox would travel as the last leg of his trip when he visited Devil John, is in fact, the actual "trail" referred to in "The Trail of the Lonesome Pine." If one travels southwest on Main Street, in Pound, after crossing highway 23, the road (state route T-630) becomes Old North Fork Road. This roadway, from the town limit to Horse Gap is what remains of the actual trail described in "The Trail of the Lonesome Pine!"

In the same regard, it is the geographical proximity of Pound "Gap" to Devil John's Virginia home that is used in Fox's description of "Lonesome Cove" to Fox's fictionalized town of The "Gap." In short, the actual "trail" of the "Lonesome Pine" laid, not between Big Stone Gap and a fictional, mountain homestead (as is generally believed), but between the modern town of Pound and what remains of Devil John Wright's land at Horse Gap just outside the town limit.

While it is simple historical fact that Fox's character of Devil Judd Tolliver is based on Devil John, the physical description of Devil Judd may be more remarkable than one may think. Fox describes Devil Judd as being a "giant." Interpretations of the Devil Judd character have usually been of a large, stocky, robust and bearded mountain man. This would be the visage created by the quintessential Devil Judd Tolliver portrayed so well by Tommy Masters, of Big Stone Gap in his years with the outdoor drama. In reality, Fox's description, exemplified by illustrations in the original publication, is of a proportionately built man with gauntly thin facial features comparable to a bird of prey. It is an accurate description of Devil John . . . except for the references to his giant stature.

John Fox Jr. knew Devil John from his mid-fifties up to his mid-seventies. John was indeed a tall, somewhat lanky figure, being just over six feet tall, even as an older man --- but he was no giant. What may be so remarkable about this is, rather than being just a literary device used to convey Jack Hale's courage in dealing with the giant Devil Judd, is that Devil John Wright was related to, and close with a real life "giant!"

It may be recalled that Devil John's favorite uncle was the proportionately built, seven foot, eleven inch tall circus attraction, the "Kentucky River Giant," Martin Van Buren Bates. This close relation, and all the exceptional tales that it undoubtedly possessed, being such an important part of Devil John's life, was probably not lost on an accomplished writer such as John Fox Jr. Unfortunately, it's a proposition which can't be conclusively proven. However, it seems to be more than coincidence that a main character developed by an author as adept as Fox at blending plural sources into the singular, described as a giant, would just happen to be based on a man actually related to a genuine giant   Therefore, the contention that the character of Devil Judd Tolliver's stature was inspired by Devil John's real life giant uncle just might be viewed as more obvious inference than sheer conjecture.

The "Daves"

In the novel, Jack Hale's nemesis and rival for June's affections is her cousin, "young" Dave Tolliver. Young Dave is presented as the son of another of Devil Judd's brothers referred to as "Ol' Dave Tolliver. The reader is led to understand a backstory of a "falling out" occurring between Devil Judd and his older brother, Ol' Dave, prior to the story's beginning. In as much as unraveling John Fox Jr.'s inspiration and sources regarding Devil John Wright, his kin and the region's history is concerned, here's where things get a little murky.

Devil John Wright did have four brothers. However, none of these were older than Devil John, and none were named Dave. Likewise, none of Devil John's brothers had a son named Dave, and the only one who named his son after him was Samuel Wright. It has already been ascertained that Samuel Wright, "Kinky Haired" Sam, is the basis for the character of "Uncle Billy," and there was no falling out between Devil John and this brother in the novel, or in real life. A comparison of "Kinky Haired" Sam's son reveals no corresponding attributes to the young Dave character. Further complicating any attempt at identifying Hale's rival, young Dave, with any actual counterpart in the Wright family, is the fact that the young Dave character's father, Ol Dave, can actually be identified with a well-known historical figure. This would be the real life person, and infamous murder victim, Ol' Ira Mullins. In Fox's novel Ol Dave is murdered by the only character in the story called by his real life name. This would be the wonderfully creepy, but accurately portrayed backwoods sorcerer and outlaw known as the "Red Fox." History records that Swedenborgian holy man, renown herb doctor and cold-blooded killer "Doc" M. B. Taylor, simply known as "The Red Fox," was convicted and hanged for the murders of Ol' Ira Mullins and members of his family in 1893.

The Red Fox, along with two accomplices, laid in wait as Ol' Ira and his kin traveled by a place that would later become known as the "killing Rock" at the crest of Black Mountain. It was here, near the Virginia, Kentucky border, that Ol' Ira was ambushed as he sat in a "jolt" wagon which, being unable to walk, he was forced to travel in. The poor man didn't have a chance. The only two survivors, including Ol Ira's son, easily identified the Red Fox as the leader of the assassins.

While it seems that O'l Ira's son should be able to be linked to the young Dave Tolliver character, this is problematic. The boy did not share Ira's first name (his name was John Mullins), and he was only fourteen years old at the time. This seems much too young to match up with the young Dave character's portrayal in Fox's novel.

To date no relative of, or any person contemporary with Devil John Wright can be matched with the character of young Dave Tolliver. It seems that this major character is either based on some actual person known only to John Fox Jr., thus lost to history, or is wholly a fictional construct of the author's imagination. The latter contention is bolstered by the fact that, by the novel's end, the young Dave character is conveniently killed off while "out west," a demise which presently can't be attributed to any known person.

"Bub Tolliver"

As to the minor character, June's little brother "Bub," there does seem to be a corresponding, real life person the character could've been derived from. Bub is described as a young boy who is either a brother, or step-brother to the heroine June Tolliver. The short-syllabled nickname, "Bub," is a common one throughout Appalachia, and the South in general. While no actual ages for any of the main characters in the novel are given, a range for some, especially June, can be estimated from the story's narrative.

It seems that at the beginning of the approximate decade that unfolds in the book, June Tolliver is first introduced as an adolescent of about fourteen to sixteen years old. This leaves an impression of little Bub Tolliver as being somewhere between eight and eleven years old. This makes for a criteria of a real life son of Devil John of about ten years of age that John Fox Jr. would've encountered when visiting his friend's home. Such a young boy would be expected to have a short-syllabled nickname with which everyone in the Wright household referred to him. Is there any corresponding, real life person? The answer is, yes!

Devil John Wright did have one son of particular notoriety, and is the most likely source for the character of Bub Tolliver. This person was born in 1898, making him exactly ten years old when "The Trail of the Lonesome Pine" was published. John Fox Jr. Would've actually watched this young man grow up! Due to another, younger sibling's inability to accurately pronounce his first name, this man was known all his life by an unusual, short-syllabled nickname. This was the illustrious William T. Wright, whose little sister mispronounced his first name as "Chid-dum" instead of William. Thus he was, and continues to be simply known as, "Chid!"

Chid Wright would grow to become a highly educated, prominent civic leader, teacher, administrator and renowned author of the memoir of his father, whom he loyally cared for until his death. As previously mentioned, William "Chid" Wright published "Devil John Wright of the Cumberlands" in 1970. If John Fox Jr. Relied on any real life source for the character of "Bub" Tolliver, "Chid" Wright seems to be the obvious choice.

June's Stepmother

June Tolliver's stepmother is a minor character in the story. Her real name is never given, she is simply referred to as a "stepmother." Why Fox failed to "flesh-out" this character is not known, but her description makes it obvious that she is based on an actual person.

She is portrayed as being reticent in conversation, but given to verbal, and physical abusiveness when angered. She lives with Devil Judd, but is not June's real mother. With the exception of performing rudimentary chores, she is presented as being bedridden. The inference should be obvious by the portrayal. The stepmother character is, undoubtedly, based on Devil John's first, legal wife, Mattie Humphrey Wright!

Consider the following. The stepmother would be based on a real life spouse of Devil John Wright. She would've been present in the household on Elkhorn Creek during the time-frame spanning the years of Devil John's friendship with Fox. This would include her living presence at the 1908 publication date of "The Trail of the Lonesome Pine." Children, such as that portrayed by June, who were fathered by her husband with other women are within her charge. With the exception of being capable of performing menial physical tasks, she stays in her bed. She is given to violent outbursts. This person is portrayed as having little quality of life and very limited social interaction.

If, as has been proposed, Devil John's wife, Mattie, indeed suffered from some sort of mental illness or dementia; Fox's description of the stepmother based on Mattie would be an accurate one. It is this description, taken to be based on the poor woman's real life circumstance, which further bolsters the previously stated contention that Mattie Wright was actually a mentally disabled individual.

It is an unfortunate fact that, rather than being more precisely portrayed as simply incapable, the stepmother character comes off as the stereotypical, lazy, "hillbilly" matriarch. It is an unintended consequence of such characterization, on Fox's part, that would later be reflected by the unflattering, clichéd portrayals of mountain mothers in such works as the "Li'l Abner" comic strip and Hollywood's "Ma Kettle." Mattie Wright passed away seventeen years after being thus immortalized by Fox's stepmother character. As previously stated, the cause of her death was listed simply as "senility."

The "Falins"

The Falin clan, also called the "Red Falins," is the arch-enemy of the Tolliver clan, also referred to as the "Black Tollivers." One of the book's major themes incorporates the ongoing, family feud between the Tollivers, headed by Devil Judd, and the Falins, headed by "Ol' Buck" Falin. It is well known, and accepted that this feud is based on the actual Wright-Jones feud of the mid 1880's.

The corresponding history of the Wright-Jones feud with "The Trail of the Lonesome Pine's" portrayal of the Tolliver - Falin feud is an easy one. If Devil Judd is accepted as being based on Devil John, there is only one candidate for the feud portrayed in the novel. This is the Wright-Jones feud that would've been related to, if not witnessed firsthand by, Fox during his friendship with Devil John.

Based on this, the character of "Ol' Buck" Falin, in the book, is easily associated with Devil John's real life nemesis, "Ol' Clabe" Jones. Likewise, the Falins are, undoubtedly, based upon the Jones clan of Knott County, Kentucky.

"Bad" Rufe Tolliver

There is absolutely no doubt whatsoever that Fox's murderous character, "Bad" Rufe Tolliver, is based on none other but "Bad" Talt Hall! The corresponding historical facts of "Bad" Talt's life with the portrayal of "Bad" Rufe are unassailable. Indeed, it is the unfortunate demise of "Bad" Talt Hall (and the "Red Fox") that reveals the time-frame for the story of "The Trail of the Lonesome Pine." It is the known execution date of "Bad" Talt from which can be extrapolated, using the novel's narrative, the span of years within which "The Trail of the Lonesome Pine" actually takes place.

"Bad" Talt, though not a relative, was a constant figure in the Wright household. As such, he was well known, even feared by Devil John's children. Accordingly, Fox portrays "Bad" Rufe as not being a blood relative to the main character June Tolliver. In the book she refers to him as a "foster uncle" whom she feared.

At the beginning of the novel "Bad" Rufe has been sent "out west" by Devil Judd in order to quell the ongoing hostilities between the Tollivers and the Falins. Likewise, at the behest of Devil John Wright, "Bad" Talt Hall traveled westward to Memphis, Tennessee to relieve tensions during the Wright-Jones feud.

It was upon Hall's return to the region that he committed the crime for which he was hanged. As previously stated, "Bad" Talt Hall murdered police Chief, James Hylton in the town of Norton, Virginia. This is the event portrayed in "The Trail of the Lonesome Pine" of "Bad" Rufe gunning down Guard Sergeant Mockaby at the town of the "Gap." Thus the town of Norton is included as a source for Fox's fictional town in the novel.

In the book "Bad" Rufe's trial occurs in the "Gap." Here the outlaw is convicted on the dramatic testimony by the heroine, June Tolliver. He is sentenced to hang by the jury. It is a novel addition to the outdoor drama, performed every summer in Big Stone Gap, that audience members are placed on stage as jury members in the drama's rendition of "Bad" Rufe's trial!

As he stands on the gallows, also portrayed as being constructed at the "Gap," one of Devil Judd's clansmen attempts to shoot "Bad" Rufe from a hidden sniper's nest. This was in order to keep Devil Judd's promise that no Tolliver "would ever be hanged." Unfortunately for "Bad" Rufe, the sniper's bullet merely wings him. Thus gravely wounded, he meets his end kicking at the hangman's noose!

The reality is that "Bad" Talt was jailed, tried and executed, not in Big Stone Gap, but in the newly formed county seat of Wise, Virginia. It may be recalled that Wise had been called Gladeville during the Civil War. It is "Bad" Talt's incarceration, trial and execution that allows the town of Wise to be included in Fox's depiction of the "Gap." As of a matter of fact, previously dealt with, "Bad" Talt Hall was the first person to ever be executed in Wise County, Virginia. He was hanged on September 2, 1892.

Just as the novel is concerned with Devil Judd Tolliver allowing any of his kin to be hanged, the community had very real concerns as to whether or not Devil John Wright would allow his best friend to be executed. Newspapers as far east as Lynchburg, Virginia echoed those concerns by reporting that the "infamous outlaw," Devil John Wright, and his "gang," would attempt to break Hall out of the jail by "violence." As a result, more than fifty extra guards were placed at the jail and adjoining gallows on the day of the hanging!

Instead of a last minute, violent reprieve, neither Devil John, who was not present at the execution, nor any of his kin attempted any jailbreak. Devil John sent inquiry to his old comrade asking if "Bad" Talt wished to be buried in Kentucky. This dashed any last hope Hall may have had regarding any rescue. "Bad" Talt Hall met a grisly end, having his life slowly strangled away for a reported seventeen minutes by the noose. Devil John sent a wagon for his friend's body, and buried Thomas Talton ("Bad" Talt) Hall in his own family's cemetery, where he would also bury two of his sons, and his wife, and lifelong companion, Mattie!

June Tolliver

Named for her birth month, June Tolliver, Fox's most famous character, is the heroine and main character of "The Trail of the Lonesome Pine." As such, John Fox Jr. portrays her in two distinct ways. First, she is depicted as the teenaged daughter of Devil Judd Tolliver. She is described as being "like a little, wild animal" when originally encountered by the "civilized" engineer, Jack Hale, at the base of the "Lonesome Pine." Hale, the cosmopolitan "furriner," is immediately smitten by the wily, barefooted nymph in her in little red dress. He will, eventually, sponsor her relocation to the Gap, where she receives education, social training and clothing available in turn-of-the-century Appalachia.

As the story progresses, June is sent to Lexington, Kentucky for higher education. Here, she resides with Hale's sister. Eventually, she is sent to New York City where the metamorphosis from backwoods scamp to sophisticated young lady is completed. It is this refined, beautiful and educated sophisticate that is Fox's secondary portrayal of June Tolliver. The resemblance of this second incarnation of June Tolliver to John Fox Jr.'s real life love interest, the Austrian operatic diva, and New Yorker, Fritzi Scheff, cannot be denied!

Of course, this becomes the ultimate irony of the novel. As June is transformed into a full-fledged, sophisticated lady-about-town, Hale descends more and more into uncivilized Appalachian-styled austerity back home in the Gap. By the story's end, the novel's two main characters, still embroiled in their romance, have virtually reversed their respective roles. Under such ironical circumstance, can their love be reconciled? You'll have to read the book to find out!

It is the first portrayal of June that can be explored for a corresponding, real life figure as part of the character's basis, in regard to Devil John Wright. The primary criteria can be based on one simple contention. June is the biological daughter of Devil Judd Tolliver. Devil Judd is based on Devil John. Therefore, June Tolliver must be based, in part, on a real life daughter of Devil John Wright that John Fox Jr. would've encountered (and was apparently, indelibly impressed with) during his many visits to Devil John's home.

Adding to a criteria of a corresponding real life daughter of Devil John's, and narrowing the choices, would be June's depicted age. As previously stated, the heroine June gives damning testimony at "Bad" Rufe's trial, resulting in his conviction and subsequent hanging. It is known that the actual event corresponding to this is the trial and execution of "Bad" Talt Hall. These events actually took place in 1892. The novel's narrative spans a time-frame of, approximately, eight years from June's introduction to the trial. She is originally portrayed as an adolescent of fourteen to sixteen years old. This results in a twenty-two to twenty-four year old June Tolliver testifying at her "foster uncle's" trial By simply doing the math, working backwards, an approximate birth year for whichever of Devil John's daughters June is based upon can be calculated.

This would be a span between the late 1860's up to 1870 for a possible birth year of any real life daughter of Devil John's to be a basis for the June Tolliver character. Preferably this would include a daughter born in the month of June, or possessing a first name that might precipitate Fox choosing to change the actual name to June. In regard to the daughters of Devil John, there seems to actually be two candidates meeting the birth year, and other historical criteria for June Tolliver!

Now, there have long been those who, for whatever reasons, have maintained that Fox's heroine is a completely fictional construct. It's hard to see how this can be the case. John Fox

Jr. seems to employ the "local color genre" style of blending plural, real life sources in virtually all of his characterizations. This was done with few, if any, exceptions. For example, in regard to June, the character is portrayed as having blonde hair. While it is true that none of Devil John's daughters had blonde hair . . . Fox's wife, Fritzi Scheff, was famously blonde headed! It must be remembered, "The Trail of the Lonesome Pine" was actually dedicated to Fritzi Scheff. The contention that John Fox Jr.'s most famous character, June Tolliver, is completely "made-up" seems to be unfounded.

Beyond all of this, there is an additional, somewhat disconcerting, factor that must be included in the criteria of a real life daughter of Devil John's being an inspiration for June Tolliver. Consider the following excerpt taken from the February 5th, 1931 memorial article, regarding Devil John, appearing in "The Mountain Eagle" newspaper in Letcher County, Kentucky.

"During the day on Sunday as many as two thousand people visited the old home of John Wright, attended the funeral services and viewed the remains. People who knew him came from hundreds of miles distant. His daughter, June, one of John Fox's characters, came in from Pennsylvania."

The reason for this, seemingly conclusive, report being somewhat disconcerting regarding a real life source for Fox's character is four-fold. First, none of Devil John's daughters were named "June." Second, all of the children of Devil John, in attendance at his funeral, were photographed posing by his casket. The newspaper article goes on to report this photographing of his children. The problem is that all of those in the picture are easily identified. None of the women meet any reasonable criteria for June, and none of them were from Pennsylvania! Thirdly, there is absolutely no report or tradition, within the Wright family, of any of Devil John's daughters being the basis for June Tolliver Much less would be the lack of report or tradition of the presence of such a person at his funeral within the family. The family simply made no such claim. Lastly, this excerpt is taken from the same article where some facts regarding Devil John are made, which may be erroneous. This would include the previously addressed contention of Devil John's presence at the Battle of Shiloh during the Civil War. The article's contention, however, simply can't be ignored, and is cautiously added here.

The first daughter of Devil John Wright that may be a contender as the inspiration for June Tolliver, is a woman named Easter Wright. While Easter would not have been a teenager when first encountered by John Fox Jr., being born in 1884, she would've been June's depicted age at the 1908 publication of the book. Her name, "Easter," with its Spring-like connotation, can't be ignored as being so proximal to the Spring-like name of "June!"

The second contender for Fox's inspiration is the seldom referred to, virtually unknown, daughter fathered by Devil John with Margaret Austin. This daughter is the somewhat mysterious Mahala Wright. This person is mysterious because there are only a couple of, almost off-handed, references to her in the historical record. Beyond her name, birth mother and birthdate of February 7th, 1865, her death in 1899 and her marriage to Henry Mullins --- there is a conspicuous lack of any mention, oral tradition, or facts in the family history regarding her.

Her inclusion as a possible basis for the June Tolliver character is twofold. First, and foremost, she is the one and only daughter by Devil John that fits the criteria of being a teenager when Fox could've first encountered her. Mahala was born in 1865. This would've made the girl about nineteen years old when Fox could've presumably met her around 1885. Obviously, this renders an age within a couple of years of that depicted in the June Tolliver character. This is especially true when the date of the trial, and June's dramatized testimony, is considered. Mahala, whose name is a Creek Indian word meaning beautiful, would've been the one and only daughter of Devil John's in their mid, to late twenties, just as June is portrayed, during the 1892 trial.

Secondly, would be the name Mahala itself. It is doubtful that Fox would've considered such a uniquely Native American name to be a good fit for his heroine. It can only be surmised that Fox wouldn't confuse his readers, who still held strong, negative biases against Native Americans, by depicting his main character with her real Native American first name of Mahala.

All possible inference and possible coincidence aside, Mahala Wright remains the best candidate, based on the necessary criteria, among Devil John's daughters to be the actual inspiration for June Tolliver. Perhaps she either failed to be (or refused to be) photographed with her siblings, at her father's funeral. It is known that Devil John's funeral was somewhat controversial, for various reasons, amongst some of his children. Many simply refused to even attend their father's interment. Perhaps Mahala was among them. Regardless, the mystery surrounding Mahala Wright's life endures, as it does for the indomitable June Tolliver!

The Lonesome Pine

The final aspect of "The Trail of the Lonesome Pine" to be explored is the novel's namesake, the "Lonesome Pine" itself. Some maintain that the Lonesome Pine was merely a romantic plot device. There never was any such tree. Some have scanned the many ridges encircling Big Stone Gap, Virginia in hopes of spying the tell-tale crown of the tree towering above all others. Others claim it resided at the summit of Pine Mountain in Letcher County, Kentucky. Still others have asserted that it existed farther west in Kentucky's Bluegrass Region. It has even been reported as being somewhere in Tennessee's Smoky Mountains. Was there ever a real Lonesome Pine? Can we know where it originally was? Can we ascertain its current whereabouts? Incredible as it may seem, the answer to all of these questions is a resounding . . . yes!

The famous tree is described, in Fox's novel, as standing like a conspicuously tall, lone sentinel at the summit of a mountain. At the base of this mountain is located the Tolliver homestead in "Lonesome Cove" on "Lonesome Creek" both ostensibly named for the "Lonesome Pine." The opposite side of this mountain faces a large gap in the opposing ridge of mountains. Within this gap lay the small, mountain community known as "The Gap," from which the giant evergreen could be seen by all.

It is his curiosity regarding such an improbable landmark (most trees atop windy mountains can't grow very tall) that evokes newcomer to the "Gap," engineer, Jack Hale, to climb the "trail" leading from The Gap to the auspicious tree. Simultaneously, a young mountain girl named June Tolliver has sneaked from Lonesome Cove to climb to the tree. Here she views The Gap, and considers the big, unknown world laying beyond the little town, represented by the endless, rolling ridges stretched to the horizon. It is the unlikely meeting of Jack and June, at the Lonesome Pine, that sparks the timeless, romantic story unveiled in the novel.

When John Fox Jr. And Devil John began their friendship, Devil John maintained no less than two homes. The primary of these would be the home on Elkhorn Creek, in Letcher County, Kentucky. As stated, here Devil John's only neighbors were his brother, Samuel, and his wife, Martha, who ran a grist mill off of the creek. This is undoubtedly the basis for the Tolliver homestead, presented in the novel as Lonesome Cove, on Lonesome Creek. However, this can't be considered as the location for the Lonesome Pine. There is no mountain just above the home where one could climb to view an opposing, mountain gap. There is no adjacent town to be viewed even if such a peak existed.

The second, notable home maintained by Devil John, and where Fox would spend the majority of time visiting, was located just outside the modern day town of Pound in Wise County, Virginia. Here Devil John's home was situated by a creek, at the base of the mountain forming the eastern flank of Horse Gap. At the top of the peak above Devil John's home, one is presented with a view of an opposing mountain gap, the town laying within that gap, and endless, rolling ridges stretching to the horizon The mountain above Devil John's old home-place, at Horse Gap, just outside the town previously known as "The Pound Gap," is littered, like no other adjoining peak . . . with pine trees!

While Devil John was aware of the celebrity accorded to him by "The Trail of the Lonesome Pine," he, reportedly, never read the book that was his greatest claim to fame. During the novel's initial popularity Devil John simply remained involved in land dealing, law enforcement and, unfortunately, logging on his property. He simply did not realize that standing atop the land he owned at Horse Gap stood one of the most famous pieces of lumber in American history . . . the Lonesome Pine!

An article released by the Associated Press, upon the death of Devil John in 1931, contains an excerpt from an interview conducted with him at the home at Horse Gap, just outside Pound, Virginia. It reads as follows:

"Though "Devil Judd" Tolliver was inspired by his own character, Wright never read "The Trail of the Lonesome Pine" or any of Fox's books. Often he would guide callers to where the lonesome pine had stood. "Son," he once told a reporter, "the lonesome pine was cut down and sawed into lumber. Some of it was used for beams in that old water mill you might have seen down there at the side of Pound Village."

While John Fox Jr. relied upon Devil John's Kentucky home on Elkhorn Creek for the inspiration regarding details of the fictional "Lonesome Cove;" it is the pine tree studded peak on the outskirts of Pound, Virginia that was the actual location of the very real Lonesome Pine! Likewise, it is doubtful that few, if any, of the townspeople residing in Pound, Virginia realize that their town (formerly called "The Pound Gap") is a major inspiration for Fox's "The Gap" in the novel! Regardless, it is Pound, Virginia where the legendary Lonesome Pine once stood, and inspired one of the most enduring works of literature in American history!

Fittingly, it is on the peak forming the western flank of Horse Gap, directly opposite from where the mighty tree once stood, that a small cemetery can be found. **Here is the final resting place of "Devil" John Wesley Wright, now eternally on the real. . . "Trail" of the real…"Lonesome Pine!"**

Made in the USA
Middletown, DE
09 February 2023

24394687R10038